NO MATTER
- WHAT -

Torn Curtain Publishing
Wellington, New Zealand
www.torncurtainpublishing.com

© Copyright 2021 Ginette Edmonds. All rights reserved.
ISBN Softcover 9780473594183

No portion of this book may be reproduced, stored in a retrieval system or transmitted in any form or by any means—electronic, mechanical, photocopy, recording or otherwise—except for brief quotations in printed reviews of promotion, without prior written permission from the author.

All details included in this book are written from the author's best recollection and perspective. Names of people included in this book are used with permission. Some names and places have been changed to preserve anonymity. This book is not intended as a substitute for professional counselling or advice.

Unless otherwise indicated, all Scripture quotations are taken from the Holy Bible, New Living Translation, copyright © 1996, 2004, 2015 by Tyndale House Foundation. Used by permission of Tyndale House Publishers, Inc., Carol Stream, Illinois 60188. All rights reserved.

Scripture quotations marked NIV are taken from the Holy Bible, New International Version®, NIV®. Copyright © 1973, 1978, 1984, 2011 by Biblica, Inc.™ Used by permission of Zondervan. All rights reserved worldwide. www.zondervan.com. The "NIV" and "New International Version" are trademarks registered in the United States Patent and Trademark Office by Biblica, Inc.™

Scriptures marked NKJV are taken from the New King James Version®. Copyright © 1982 by Thomas Nelson. Used by permission. All rights reserved.

Scripture quotations marked TPT are from The Passion Translation®. Copyright © 2017, 2018 by Passion & Fire Ministries, Inc. Used by permission. All rights reserved. ThePassionTranslation.com.

Cover Photo: Ginette Edmonds with Pansee Sangserm in Thailand. Used with Permission.

Cataloguing in Publishing Data
Title: No Matter What
Author: Ginette Edmonds
Subjects: Christian Missions, Thailand, Inner healing, Spiritual Growth
Typeset in Palantino Linotype and Poppins.

A copy of this title is held at the National Library of New Zealand.

NO MATTER
- WHAT -

TWO DECADES OF GOD'S
FAITHFULNESS IN THAILAND

GINETTE EDMONDS
With Averil Bennett

In memory of Mum and Dad who always believed in me and were a constant support and encouragement whilst I was serving God in Thailand. They stirred up many, many people to pray.

For my brother Edwin and his wife Airini who accepted me into their family and provided a listening ear along with wrap-around prayer and practical provision not only throughout my years in Thailand, but also on my return.

For Edwin's children and families who I love as my own.

Contents

Foreword		*ix*
Author's Note		*xi*
Acknowledgements		*xiii*
Prologue		1
Chapter 1	Childhood Challenges	5
Chapter 2	Called to Serve	13
Chapter 3	Led by Love	21
Chapter 4	Strategic Redirection	31
Chapter 5	Spiritual Awakening	37
Chapter 6	Anchored in God	47
Chapter 7	Facing Oppression	57
Chapter 8	Walking in Authority	67
Chapter 9	Darkness and Despair	79
Chapter 10	Healing and Restoration	91
Chapter 11	Back to Bangkok	105
Chapter 12	Coming Home	113
Epilogue		123

FOREWORD

Ginette went to Thailand because she believed that she was called to be a missionary nurse, only to find after her arrival that this was no longer possible. God's call certainly was to Thailand, as the years that followed have illustrated, but his purposes were much wider and deeper than she could have possibly understood as her sense of call was developing. God often leads us through a number of different roles and ministries as our gifts develop, sometimes through difficult events and circumstances. The way Ginette handled these, underlines her strong desire to know God and do his will, a trait which has been evident throughout the time we have known her.

Ginette became a member of the OMF (Overseas Missionary Fellowship) team in Central Thailand, where we were already serving. As fellow Kiwis, we enjoyed sharing our experiences and learning about the work together. What a privilege it was to be involved in starting churches where none have ever existed before. Thailand is a Buddhist country—it is commonly stated that to be Thai, is to be Buddhist. It is a country where each person must earn their own success in life, the prevailing philosophy being, "do good, get good; do bad, get bad." It is also a country where people live in great fear of evil spirits. Satan is our enemy, and he does not want to see people turning to faith in God, so he attacks both the local people and those who have come to share the good news.

In a very honest way, Ginette shares her experience of working as a single missionary in the Thai environment. Her strong desire has always been to know God and do his will, and to help others grow in their relationship with God and become members of a church group in their local area.

Serving God in Thailand has rarely led to dramatic or rapid church growth. Humanly speaking, it has often seemed discouraging and depressing work, and yet churches continue to be established across that kingdom.

This book brings to light many aspects of the spiritual battle in a culture and worldview where a biblical understanding of God as the Creator and Saviour is unknown. Ginette gives us a summary of the many lessons she has learnt and how God has been faithful to sustain her throughout this period, 1979–2001.

Ian and Maybeth Roberts
Whangarei, NZ

AUTHOR'S NOTE

Year after year friends urged me to write a book with all my stories from Thailand. *Me? A book?* The idea seemed beyond the realm of possibility. Then, in November 2019, I went on a three-week mission trip to Nepal. Walking to various meetings, my team members and I had plenty of time to chat, and because the context was so similar to what I had experienced in Thailand, I began to share many of my stories. Again, the comment came, "You should write a book." This time, I began to think about it more seriously. "Lord if you want me to write a book, please show me how," I prayed.

On my return to New Zealand, I took a course by Brian Simmons called 'Unlocking your Book'. I thought that if I was ever going to do it, this would be a great help. The first thing I learned was that I needed to deal with my negative inner voice. This was very helpful, as it was exactly where I was stuck! As the course proceeded and I began to say yes to God, I found the memories began to flow.

My desire in writing this book is to show how God took me as a fearful introvert, and through many years of challenging experiences, showed me that he is reliable. Having learnt to experience God's lovingkindness and favour as my norm, I can testify that anyone can step out in obedience to God and find him trustworthy!

ACKNOWLEDGEMENTS

I wish to acknowledge the friends God has wonderfully and strategically provided to help me along the way.

Averil Bennett, my fellow OMF'er. You came along as an answer to prayer for help in the writing of this book. The insights you offered shifted my perspectives on what God was doing, both in my own life and during my time in Thailand. Thank you for giving a whole year to journeying with me in the writing of this book.

Elizabeth Brown. You have been my confidante, and checker of all my materials for twenty-five years. What an amazing labour of love!

Jennie Hamlin. Thank you for your wise friendship, and for the expertise you brought to the early edition of my manuscript.

To all my friends who have given me encouragement and advice along the way: thank you for enabling me to keep going when I thought, "I can't do this!"

To those who have mentored me throughout my life—there are too many of you to mention by name, but I am grateful for each one. You have loved me unconditionally, had faith in me, encouraged me and drawn out the best in me throughout my journey of transformation.

To all my Thai friends who have made this book possible. In sharing people's stories, I have often changed names or situations to protect you, but you will recognise your own story. Thank you for sharing your lives with me, for being such great friends, and for helping me to understand Thai culture. I thank God for each of you, and for his grace I see poured out in you.

To the OMF prayer teams throughout New Zealand. I owe you a great debt. Your prayer support has made a huge difference. In particular, to the team in Christchurch. Thank you for the opportunity to journey together in mutual friendship for forty-three years!

To Anya McKee and the Torn Curtain Publishing team. Thank you for your wisdom and expertise in editing my manuscript. I am truly humbled by your ability to draw out the gold in my story. Your prophetic insights have enabled me to see my story through God's eyes, and released me from the burden of insecurity and failure I carried over many years. Thank you too for creating a delightful cover design and producing a truly lovely book. Working with you has been a highlight of my writing journey.

Most of all I owe my deepest gratitude to Jesus who alone made all this possible.

PROLOGUE

Classical music played and sweet incense wafted over us as we sat in the temple's funeral alcove. The monks had just finished chanting in the ancient *Pali* language, which no one understood, although the Thai inscriptions on their fans gave a clear message: "No life. No return. No hope. No resurrection." The bereaved family started to 'make merit' by serving the monks a meal.

Somchai and his father were new Christians, two of very few in their family. When Somchai's father died, the family had demanded his Buddhist funeral be held in the temple he had helped build before he became a Christian. Somchai had asked if we would conduct a short Christian ceremony for his father following the Buddhist rituals, and we had agreed. Now the family had begun serving the meal, and Somchai indicated to us that this would be a good time to start. As our tiny group began to sing *How Great Thou Art*, an amazing sense of God's presence and majesty filled the place. But when Udom Chuduang, a visiting pastor, stood to speak a few words he had prepared for the occasion, we were suddenly startled by a commotion outside. We tried to carry on and take no notice of the shouting and scuffling that had erupted, but when someone entered the temple saying, "Tell that speaker to stop! There's a man with a gun outside and he wants to kill him!", it became increasingly obvious that someone (or something) was not happy about the fact that Christians were worshipping in a Buddhist temple.

We had been praying that God's glory would be revealed through this funeral, yet suddenly our pastor's life was in danger. In that moment, Arlene, my new fellow worker, was sure we were going to die. In fact, we were all fearful of what might happen next. But, clinging to the promise that God would always be with us, I encouraged Pastor Udom to speak on.

Miraculously, we finished the ceremony unharmed, and returned to the house for a meal together. We spent a long time in prayer that day—for God's covering and protection over Somchai's family, that he would open the eyes of those who were at the funeral, and that God would bless the people we had come to serve.

We were surprised, however, when the following week, three of the people who had so violently opposed Pastor Udom's message experienced serious accidents. Word soon spread that the gunman who had threatened us was shot dead the very next day. Two other men had shouted in blasphemous opposition against God—one was struck by lightning a few days later and killed, while the other had a serious stroke and was paralysed. Having heard the news, Somchai told his family and relatives that they did not have to believe in God, but warned them that they should not blaspheme Him, or bad things would happen to them.

Of course, the incident was intended to stir up fear, and as a naturally fearful person, I once again found myself turning to the promises of God for protection and encouragement as I put my trust and confidence in him. God had constantly affirmed his loving acceptance of me as his friend whom he had chosen to serve him, and I had learned that he was always there for me, no matter what the situation. Now, however, I needed to look again to him and to hold onto the specific promise he had given me for this funeral, and indeed for my time in Thailand:

> *But you my servant Israel, Jacob, whom I've chosen, seed of my beloved friend Abraham. I drew you to myself from the ends of the earth and called you from its farthest corner. I say to you. You are my servant; I have chosen you and not rejected you! Do not yield to fear, for I am always near. Never turn your gaze from me, for I am your faithful God. I will infuse you with my strength and help you in every situation. I will hold you firmly with my victorious right hand.*
> Isaiah 41:8-10 TPT

As I leaned on his promise, God indeed gave me his strength—even when I felt overwhelmingly weak and had no idea what to do. Once again, all I had to do was to turn to him in prayer. He had never failed to be there for me, no matter what kind of situation I found myself in, and he would be with me throughout the days to come. He always was, and always will be, my faithful God. And yet, I still find it extraordinary that I should have been in Thailand at all! Looking back to my childhood, I could never have imagined ending up in such an alarming situation in such a far-away country!

Chapter One

Childhood Challenges

I'm sure no one could have foreseen what God had planned for my life. I was a withdrawn child who did not know how to relate to anyone, yet all I ever wanted to do was become a missionary nurse. As a young person in Bible Class, my mother had also felt the call of God to be a missionary. But when she married Dad, who was a non-Christian, she realised that her dream was not going to be fulfilled. Three years later, when I was born, my mother dedicated me to the Lord, hoping I would serve him in her place. Interestingly, she never told me this until I was in the process of applying to a mission agency.

As children, Mum took me and my brother Edwin, who was three years younger than me, to Sunday School, where we learnt about Jesus and his love for us and for the whole world. Enticed by book prizes, we eagerly took part in annual scripture memory competitions. My prizes were always books about missionaries. I remember loving the one about Mary Slessor, who worked in Africa. The front picture had her sitting under a tree in the shade teaching African children. That became my picture of what missionaries did.

Dad was totally antagonistic towards Christianity. He said he had it 'pushed down his throat' six days a week for all nine of his years at St. Andrew's boarding school in Christchurch. His parents were divorced and he felt he was sent to boarding school as punishment, that he was abandoned — as indeed he was! The result was that he acted up at school and regularly suffered under the cane. He was desperately lonely with no caring input.

Dad could be loving and kind, but he was also quite unpredictable. I could never relax when he was around. His volatility left me feeling like I was constantly walking on egg shells. Mum was always caring and very supportive, but she was quiet and withdrawn in the home. As the elder child, I felt responsible for keeping the peace in our uncertain environment. This eventually caused me to shut down; I was too scared to say anything in case it caused an explosion. Whenever this happened, I always assumed it must be my fault. I was never good enough. I could not get it right! This led to a sense of shame, fear and failure. I grew up feeling condemned and hugely lacking in confidence.

I don't remember a lot about my early primary school years except that we had a very kind new entrants' teacher. I really enjoyed her and felt safe with her. One thing I do remember is getting ringworm in my scalp and having all my hair shaved off. The shame of wearing a wig until my hair grew again certainly didn't foster any sense of self-esteem.

One day I came home from school to find Mum had all our belongings packed. She told us that she was taking Edwin and me on the interisland ferry that night. We were going to Wellington for a holiday! We were really excited because we had never travelled anywhere outside of Christchurch. She told us that because Dad was on shift work, as an ambulance driver, he had to stay behind. It was a thrilling adventure, but what we didn't know was that she was leaving Dad. She had had enough of the verbal abuse and felt she couldn't take anymore.

When Dad got home, he was frantic to find out where we had disappeared to. It took him a couple of weeks to discover where we were. Then he hurried to Wellington and found us with Mum's best friend. He begged her to come back. She absolutely refused. In turn he refused to leave until she agreed to come home.

Later, Mum told me that the day after Dad stormed in, she got up early and walked the beach pleading with God, asking him to help her. She had no desire to return. What should she do? God answered in her heart: go back for the sake of the children. It was the last thing she wanted but she knew if she obeyed God's leading, He would help her. Not much changed for her when she returned to Christchurch, but she believed God had heard and answered her prayer. We got involved with the Salvation Army and they were a great support for our family.

When I was eight years old, I was sexually abused by a teenager. This was a shocking experience. I felt unclean, unacceptable and very fearful. I shared what had happened with my mum. Poor mum—at the time it seemed like she didn't know how to help me. It was never talked about again. But the enemy was working overtime in my heart causing me to feel condemned and shameful, and as a result, I withdrew even more into myself.

Soon after this Mum started a club for me and invited girls of a similar age from the neighbourhood. Our activities together included games, handcrafts, baking and going on picnics to the beach. Mum used to work as a cake decorator, and she used her skills to make elaborate cakes and sweets for our group. I realise now this was her way of helping me to make friends and trying to bring some sense of normalcy to my life.

* * *

When I was eleven years old, Mum took me to a Billy Graham Crusade in Christchurch. It was an amazing experience with a huge crowd and powerful worship. As Billy Graham began to speak it felt like he was talking just to me:

> *To all who believed Jesus and accepted him he gave the right to become children of God.*
> *John 1:12*

This was just what my heart ached to hear. I was acceptable to someone. I was acceptable to God if I believed and received Jesus. It was that easy! Even though I felt full of sin and shame Jesus accepted me and cleansed me. How wonderful! I was very quick to go forward to invite Jesus into my life and ask him to forgive all my sins.

That night, an overwhelming sense of God's love and peace flowed over me and I knew I never wanted to lose that feeling! I was so grateful to God. From then on, Mum and I joined together in praying that Dad would come to know Jesus too, although from my child's viewpoint it looked impossible, even for God.

We attended St. Alban's Baptist Church during my last year of primary school; and the next year I joined the Bible Class. My leader became like a safe haven for me, often inviting me around for meals. My friend Lorraine and I used to babysit for her as we got older. We loved to drop in at her home for a chat after school.

I went to Papanui High School for four years and joined the weekly Christian Crusader Group. That was a great encouragement to me as I was too shy and embarrassed to relate to many other students at school. Being too nervous to ask for help resulted in me failing my School Certificate. Because nursing was my goal and 'school cert.' was essential for getting into nursing school, that meant repeating the year.

* * *

My grandfather died around that time. This was my first experience of death. Nana, a loving, caring woman who took a real interest in other people, was chronically unwell and didn't want to live on her own. So, it was decided that I would go and live with her to keep her company. Mum and Dad bought her house in Hills Road and built a flat for Nana and me to live in. She really spoilt me and loved having me stay with her. We shared a room together and she often told me of the hardships in her life. She had a strong faith in Jesus and prayed for people before she visited them. Lorraine told me she was always so encouraged when Nana had been to call on her mother. Her mother was so much happier after my Nana's visit.

Nana had a large photo in our bedroom of Jesus smiling. Children sat on his knee. I often wished I could be one of them, and at times I could almost imagine I was sitting there too. It felt awesome to be safe with Jesus.

I was baptised at the age of fifteen. That was an amazing day as I made a public declaration that I belonged to God. The minister told me to take deep breaths if I was afraid. I took so many deep breaths that I felt like I was going to pass out! When I came up out of the water, however, I had a deep sense of God's love and presence. I felt so clean. I didn't want to go to sleep that night in case I lost that incredibly precious feeling.

Dad suffered for many years with serious back pain. He could not get out of bed without help. He even needed Mum's help to get his leg over his motorbike to go to work. Over and over, I'd invite Dad to come to church with us. He'd always say, "Leave me alone; it's my only day off and I need to rest."

Then one day, an American evangelist came to our church. Dad loved Americans because he had worked with them as a paramedic on hospital ships in the Pacific during World War II, and so he agreed to attend a Saturday morning men's breakfast. When only three men turned up, the speaker took the opportunity to explain to each of the men that God was a loving Father and wanted to be their Saviour.

Dad must have thought about the message overnight. The next morning when he tried to get out of bed, spinal pain immobilised him. In that moment he cried out, "If you are real, God, please take away this back pain." Immediately he felt a wave of heat go right through his body and the pain left, never to return. He was so overjoyed that he promised God there and then that he would serve him all the days of his life. From that moment until he died at the age of ninety-one, he delighted in telling people about the wonderful love and power of Jesus to forgive and to heal. Dad was forty-eight when he turned to God. To me, this was a truly miraculous answer to my mum's persistent prayers over twenty years.

Dad's surrender to Jesus dramatically changed our family. My parents were blessed by God with a new love for each other and they began to show affection again. I was about to leave home and had been anxious for Mum's well-being, so this came as a great relief for me. For the next nine months, I lived in the Nurses' Home at St. George's Hospital while I worked as a nurse's aid in the operating theatre. Leaving home for the first time was painful, but I came home most nights just to keep the connection with my newly joyful family.

Chapter Two

CALLED TO SERVE

It was with great anticipation that I began my formal nursing training in September of 1966. The Sister-in-Charge at Christchurch Hospital met us when we arrived, and showed us to our rooms in the Nurses' Home where we would be staying for three full years. How delighted I was to find a nurse's uniform and cap neatly laid out on my bed, along with a lovely warm cape! I felt such pride. At last I had qualified for the uniform I'd admired for so many years. Finally, I was going to be a nurse! The spring daffodils were all in bloom, and my fellow student nurses and I would often go to the Avon River after class to take photos of each other in our uniforms. It was the perfect time of year to start.

For the first three months of our training, we were known as 'prelims' as we learned the basics of nursing care along with some anatomy and physiology. We enjoyed practising on dummies and on each other to gain a bit of confidence. All the tutors were kind and encouraging—in fact, the Sister-in-Charge popped in so frequently to see how we were doing that we nicknamed her 'Poppy'.

It was during this time that I discovered I loved study after all. I wanted to learn all I could about the workings of the human body, disease, treatment and nursing care. When the results of our exams were released, I was thrilled to find I had come out near the top of the class.

From that point on, we spent only one day a week in class and five days on the wards. This was ideal, as we gained plenty of practical experience and were paid for the hours we worked. My first assignment was on a men's orthopaedic ward. I was on night duty—it was a huge adjustment to sleep during the day and work at night. But the greater adjustment was learning to communicate with the patients. Many of the men were long term patients who liked nothing better than to have a bit of fun with the young nurses. One night an older man asked me to empty his urinal. He refused to hand it to me, and when I leaned over the bed to get it, he grabbed me and tried to kiss me! I was so embarrassed and scared. From then on, I tried to keep out of his way. But the ward sister knew I needed to learn to assert myself. "If you don't learn to speak to your patients then you will never make a nurse!" she told me at my first assessment.

This raised a real issue for me. At the time I had no idea why I felt so shy about speaking to people. All I knew was that I never knew what to speak about. It was always an agonising experience for me. Most of the nurses talked about where they had been with their boyfriends or what parties they'd been to, but I had only been to church or Bible Class activities on my days off. I often used to wonder how I could ever be a missionary when I couldn't even speak to people at home? I knew it would take a very great miracle.

One day as I scrubbed out bedpans in the sluice room at work, I prayed desperately for help. "I don't know what to say but I will open my mouth and trust you to put the words in it," I cried out to God. Just then a promise came to mind which I clung to:

> *I can do all things through Christ who strengthens me.*
> *Philippians 4:13 NKJV*

I still felt fearful at the thought of speaking to others but now I knew I had God's promise. I was also learning to pray for specific things and watch for his answers. One group that encouraged me greatly was the Nurses' Christian Fellowship. This was a great place to meet up with other Christians. I was especially drawn to the Sister-in-Charge of the orthopaedic ward. Her name was Margaret. Normally I wouldn't dream of talking to people of her status, but she was so friendly that she put me at ease. I told her about my heart's desire to know Jesus for myself and my longing to hear him speak to me. I also shared with her my desperate prayer to be able to relate to people.

For years I had felt envious of those who seemed to display a close relationship with God. The many leaders that I asked simply said, "read your Bible and pray." But when I tried, it seemed boring and I didn't know how to understand the Bible.

What a relief it was when Margaret offered to meet with me and disciple me! At last, I had someone to help me grow in my relationship with God. We began by meeting weekly to read the Bible together. During this time, Margaret taught me to meditate on what I was reading and to ask God what he wanted to say to me from the scriptures. The first time we did this, God spoke very clearly to me from Mark 1:16-18 (NKJV):

> *As He walked by the Sea of Galilee, He saw Simon and Andrew his brother casting a net into the sea; for they were fishermen. Then Jesus said to them, "Follow Me, and I will make you become fishers of men." They immediately left their nets and followed Him.*

Just as Jesus invited the disciples to leave their fishing, he was inviting me to follow him. I was sure of it because of his promise, "I will make you . . ." I was encouraged that this wasn't something I had to do on my own; I'd never be able to do it anyway! But this was God's invitation—that if I willingly gave up everything else to follow him, then he would transform me and enable to me to relate to others and see them come to know Jesus too.

Soon Margaret invited me to attend a weekly Bible study at her flat. This was my first introduction to a group called the Navigators, and the beginning of thirteen years' involvement in which I would learn how to become a disciple and how to disciple others. After two years, however, Margaret said to me, "You've been sitting in this group soaking everything up, but you've hardly spoken or contributed. We don't know what to do with you so we're going to change your group and put you with Sheena White." Feeling quite desperate, I pleaded with God to change me. I didn't want to be seen as a failure or be excluded from those who had helped me.

I needn't have worried. As it turned out, being placed in Sheena's group marked the beginning of a lifelong friendship. Sheena was a physiotherapist who also worked at the hospital. From the start she was kind and caring, and through her I experienced God's unconditional love. Sheena also helped me start reaching out to others and together we began a Bible study in the Nurses' Home.

At the end of my nursing training, a woman by the name of Maureen Dawson came from England to work with the Navigators. She was looking for young women to live with her for training in discipleship. I was so keen to learn that I pleaded with her to choose me. She thought I was too young, but I was so hungry to learn how to live as a Christian every day of the week, not just on Sundays, that eventually she gave in and allowed me to move in with her and her group.

* * *

By now, my training had come to an end, and I began my first job as a registered nurse in the recovery ward at the Princess Margaret Hospital in Christchurch. But the day I was due to start, I woke up feeling ill and vomiting. I picked up the phone and called to say I couldn't come to work. Later that morning when Maureen came into my room and asked what was really going on, I was petrified! How could I confess that I was unable to face the new job? That I didn't know how to relate to people? That I knew it was an opportunity to share Jesus but that I felt I was sure to fail?

What a relief to find that she was kind and accepting! I was afraid I'd be thrown out of her flat because I was inadequate for discipleship. Instead, she offered to help me learn practical ways to relate to people, like reading the newspaper to have a knowledge of general affairs, playing squash and just doing normal fun things!

Gradually she gave me the responsibility of leading a Bible study. At first, I felt like I would die because I was so scared. I could hardly speak for five minutes let alone lead a group for an hour! But Maureen encouraged me to pray and ask Jesus to give me just one person in the group to relate to, and then offer to spend time to disciple her. Amazingly, this happened! I developed a relationship with a nurse who had emotional needs and was truly grateful to have someone come alongside and help, just like I had been helped. As she grew in her understanding of how to recognise God speaking to her through the Bible and answering her prayers, she was set free from the emotional pain that had been crippling her. She then began the process of discipling another person, and with that, a passion for disciple-making was born in my life. I was learning the apostle Paul's approach:

> *But we were gentle among you, just as a nursing mother cherishes her own children. So, affectionately longing for you, we were well pleased to impart to you not only the gospel of God, but also our own lives, because you had become dear to us.*
> 1 Thessalonians 2:7-8 NKJV

After a couple of years, I sensed God calling me to move to Wellington, the capital of New Zealand to help with the Navigator work. I took a job as a public health nurse and started to disciple four university students. I also had the privilege of discipling a dental nurse who had a deep passion to grow in Jesus. These young women would come around to my flat and we'd enjoy time eating, sharing what was happening in our lives, and reading the Bible and praying together.

Three of these young women went on to have amazing discipling ministries, but when two of them did not continue with me long-term, I felt like a failure. By now I was twenty-four years old and as far as I could see, the ministry had not multiplied, but decreased. *How could God ever use me?* I wondered.

My parents were about to embark on a world trip for six weeks, and after some counselling with Maureen, I decided to join them while I specifically asked God to show me his plan for my life. Beginning the day we left New Zealand, and every day for the next three weeks, God spoke undeniably to me from the book of Isaiah:

> *I have chosen you and not rejected you.*
> Isaiah 41:9 NIV

Did this mean it was time to go to the mission field? No, it seemed instead that God was telling me: "Go back to Christchurch and be faithful in doing what you know to do — discipling others. I will bless you there." And so, when the trip was over, I returned to Christchurch where I lived for a year in a 'Navigators' flat'. This gave me enough time to be encouraged and re-establish my confidence that God could use me. Once that year was over, I was encouraged to rent a flat of my own where I could again have girls living with me for discipling.

Amazingly, God caused what seemed to be dismal inadequacy in my life, to turn around. Three young women who worked in the hospital wanted to be discipled and grow in their Christian lives, and so they moved in. Together, we prayed daily and held a weekly Bible study. We hosted evangelistic parties and even arranged to show Christian movies in the Nurses' Home, staying around to eat and chat with people afterwards.

God was so gracious. During that time a number of people came to Christ and many lifelong friends were made as we lived and ministered together. Most of those people soon got married but continued to welcome people into their lives, building caring relationships and discipling others. It had become a multiplying ministry.

Having seen God's faithfulness at work in my life, I now knew it was time to apply for missions. Now at last I was confident in God's faithfulness to use me. The promise that fortified me was:

> *The one who calls you is faithful and he will do it.*
> *1 Thessalonians 5:24 NIV*

But where, literally, should I start looking for him to 'do it'? How would I know where on earth God wanted me to serve him?

Chapter Three

LED BY LOVE

Throughout my thirteen years of nursing, I sensed God's call to be a missionary nurse, but whenever I voiced this to friends, I received the same response—that there was plenty of work to be done in New Zealand. I knew in my heart, however, that God had something else for me. At the age of twenty-seven, I began consulting God in earnest for confirmation of this call.

At Maureen's suggestion, I wrote to a number of mission societies to find out what was available. The replies heaped up and during a week with my parents at a hot springs resort, I worked through them. I asked God to lead me to a mission that did a good job of looking after their personnel. I'd heard stories of missionaries who were strapped for finance, or found themselves in very difficult situations without leaders in the country to help them, and I knew there was no way I would cope without good support. Two mission agencies seemed to be the best fit for a woman with a heart for discipling. But of course, I'd apply as a nurse—I was pretty sure that was the only reason I'd be accepted. Having narrowed down the agencies, I now began thinking about location.

I recalled a lady from my home church sharing about her experiences in Bangladesh. It had made me very frightened to hear what life was really like there. Everyone lived in gated compounds, she said; it was very difficult to have any interaction with the women in the wider Muslim community. I felt stressed just thinking about living in Bangladesh. No, I would not fit in there.

I decided instead to apply to go to India with the Navigators. However, the moment I sent the application, peace fled, and I began praying over and over, "Lord, please don't let them accept me!" What a relief when the reply came back: "Sorry, we are not taking any more single women for the time being." I was delighted! That experience helped me realise that God's peace is a bottom-line factor in his leading and guiding.

The night we came home from holiday, I continued south another two hours to stay with my best friends, Lorraine and Allan Scarlet, in a small town called Waimate. Lorraine and I had known each other since we were four years old when we were neighbours in the same street. It was a relief to pray through my turmoil with them.

The next morning as I pulled out of their circular driveway, another car swooped in behind and I noticed Lorraine signalling for me to stop. When I got out of the car and met the driver who had just pulled in, I discovered to my amazement that she was a missionary by the name of Averil Bennett. I was disappointed that I had not been able to hear her speak at a recent missions event in Christchurch, and had asked God to give me another opportunity to connect with her. Now she was here in front of me! Wow—such a coincidence had never happened to me before! I decided I'd better stay another night.

Lorraine was very hospitable and organised a lovely farm meal for us. This gave me a chance to get to know Averil. In my heart I was really excited because I knew that God had organised this, but at the same time, I had no intention of telling her what I'd been asking God about all week. I would just wait and see what God had in mind. However, Averil was very good at drawing all the information out of me—soon she discovered that I was a nurse and midwife, and with that she started telling me about a Christian hospital in Thailand that was actively looking for dedicated nurses. As she spoke about nursing in Thailand, everything she shared resonated deep in my spirit. It was exactly what I was looking for. "First," she said, "commit yourself as a missionary and second, as a nurse. And yes, discipling was seen as a vital ministry at Manorom Hospital."

Averil went on to describe the hospital's five-day working week which released nurses for outreach activities on day six. And the living arrangements sounded ideal. "Just two to three nurses make a home together in a house," Averil explained, ". . . a house on stilts, that is. That means we can entertain Thai friends."

The agency that worked in this part of the country was called OMF (Overseas Missionary Fellowship). I found out that OMF was translating Navigator Bible study books into Thai and that they were proving very successful. Averil also explained that the first nine months were spent in language school, but during that time there would be opportunities to observe hospital work, village outreach and church planting before getting assigned anywhere. She also assured me that nurses were given significant levels of responsibility in all areas of the hospital.

My heart raced with rising excitement about this possibility. It seemed to fit all the things I had been longing to do in mission work! And it seemed there was a great need for nurses. Just one year earlier there had been a horrific accident when a truck collided with the Manorom hospital van. Twelve people had been killed, including two surgeons and their families, along with nursing and medical staff, and Averil's own sister and nieces. I could see how my call was part of an answer to their desperate prayer for God to send replacement staff.

For two years I'd been asking God to show me where he wanted me to go, and with which mission. Now here was a specific opportunity presenting itself. But how could one really know? How would God make it clear whether I was to go? My heart was thumping and my mind reeling with questions about Thailand. I did not even know exactly where the country was. When Averil got out a map and pointed to Thailand, I was petrified. Right next door was Vietnam, where war was raging. All I knew was that the rest of the world expected the communist regime to take over and infiltrate the neighbouring countries.

Suddenly I had so many fears. *What if I was captured by communists? What if I was tortured? What if I died? Could I learn the Thai language when I had failed school-level French? How could I cope with eating Thai food, which I had read was so spicy that it scorched the inside of you? What about the climate?* It was as if a conflict simmered inside me with two opposing voices. Which one was God speaking? How would I ever know?

I went to bed and tried to sleep but the turmoil in my spirit made it impossible. I spent hours tossing and turning, trying to read, pray, count sheep, flicking the bedside light on and off while pros and cons jostled through my mind. About three o'clock in the morning I said to God, "I am not going anywhere unless I know it is really you. If you make it clear, I'll go anywhere with you, but I have to be sure it's you!"

In that moment I experienced the love of God baptising me all over, inside and out. It was the most glorious awareness of his presence. All the tormenting fears were washed away by a warm tangible love that flowed over me. At the same time, he spoke to my mind through scriptures that answered all my fears and concerns:

> *I am convinced that nothing can ever separate us from God's love. Neither death nor life, neither angels nor demons, neither our fears for today or our worries about tomorrow— not even the powers of hell can separate us from God's love. No power in the sky above or in the earth below - indeed, nothing in all creation will ever be able to separate us from the love of God that is revealed in Christ Jesus our Lord.*
> Romans 8:38-39

That night I knew that I would go anywhere in the world with Jesus, just to stay in his love. Having experienced the power of his presence, I fell into sleep totally at peace!

At the time I didn't recognise it, but now I understand that I was being invited into a life of intimacy with God. Intimacy was the very foundation of my sense of call—and in the years to come, it was this that gave me the ability to hang onto God through all the ups and downs of mission life and loneliness, even during the times when I had no awareness of his presence. From that night on, I simply knew that God had called me and that I would cling to his promises, no matter what.

* * *

When I woke the next morning, I immediately remembered the lesson of my traditional upbringing—that one was not supposed to base decisions on emotional experiences; that our feelings could not be relied on. And so, I said to God, "If this is really you, please confirm it."

That Sunday morning, I attended a small country church with my friends, Lorraine and Allan. Imagine my surprise when the minister stood up and said that his message that morning was from Romans chapter eight—the same passage I had been given the night before! *Surely this sort of coincidence only happened in novels,* I thought. But by the end of the service, I had clear confirmation of what the Lord had said to me.

Over lunch, I told Lorraine and Allan how I now felt sure the Lord wanted me to serve in Thailand with OMF. However, in my caution about acting on an emotional experience, I asked the Lord to continue to confirm it. "Please, Lord, could I meet a Thai?" I prayed. I knew that would be difficult because I had never heard of anyone from Thailand in my home city of Christchurch. And yet, within two weeks I had met a couple by the name of Paul and Nicky Clarke. Paul was a New Zealander married to a Thai woman. They invited me to their home for a meal. *How impossibly spicy would the food be?* I wondered. I needn't have worried. Nicky understood the local palate, and that night she made a delicious five-spice soup with eggs and pork. It was delicious.

We had an interesting conversation that night about my fears of going to Thailand and learning the Thai language. Nicky commented that she had never been to high school, yet she learnt to speak English; so she was sure God would help a better-educated Ginette learn Thai! Nicky's kindness and gentleness made a big impression on me, along with the amazing testimony of God's work in their lives as a couple. It was a great relief to meet them.

God confirmed my call further when I visited a retired couple in our church who had been missionaries in India. Mr and Mrs Enright told me about all the wonderful ways God had always provided for them financially. I returned home so encouraged that God was able to meet every need. I would never be abandoned!

By now it was obvious that I would be ignoring God's clear guidance if I did not step out in faith! And so, I applied to serve with OMF. Back came a stack of application forms to fill in, followed by an invitation to spend a weekend with the directors in Auckland. John and Joy Hewlett made me feel so at home and convinced me that OMF would be a caring mission to join. Joy shared with me about the challenges of missions and how I would face homesickness and culture shock being away from family and everything familiar. Rather than dwell on the inevitable problems, she reminded me of God's faithfulness. It did not sink in at the time as to how difficult it really would be.

I only had to wait a week when with both surprise and delight I received a letter of acceptance. And that was when all the trouble started! My initial glad response to the acceptance letter was quickly ruined when those two opposing voices re-emerged in my head, shattering my peace of mind. This was so unexpected. Was I going crazy?

One voice told me all the wrong reasons why I would go overseas and why I was not adequate for the task: *You can't find a husband so you just want to escape; You've never been to Bible College so you're not qualified; You're too shy; God will never use you.* Then the other voice, the gentle voice of the Holy Spirit, reminded me of all the ways that God had led me and affirming his call. Hearing these conflicting voices was like being blasted by an unstoppable recording. For six weeks I felt I was going insane as the crossfire raged. One day I cried out to God, "I can't stand this; I thought we were supposed to have peace when we obey you!"

That evening at church there was an altar call for anyone who wanted to follow God wholeheartedly. "Now! I must recommit my life to the Lord!" I thought. No one had made a move, but the sermon dared me to act. "Dare to be a Daniel; dare to stand alone!" I needed to go forward, no matter what.

A couple who had counselled me were surprised to see me go forward when I was already heading into overseas missions. Neither they nor I had been aware of the spiritual conflict, the intense opposition, that so often comes with such a decision. But the practical step of going forward during the altar call brought a great sense of peace. Yes, God was satisfied with my surrender. And I had discovered the power of these words:

So then, surrender to God. Stand up to the devil and resist him and he will flee.
James 4:7 TPT

Resisting the devil was a principle I had to constantly put into practice. I faced opposition from the enemy, often on a daily basis, in my thoughts. It was extremely difficult to recognise them as false because they *felt* so true! The devil accused and condemned me; he even raked up past sins and reminded me of my weaknesses and failures. It took me a long, long time to acknowledge that my negative thoughts were not from God but from the enemy. I needed to resist them by using the promises of God's Word as my truth-weapon. Only then could I renounce his lies.

But in the midst of it all, I was learning that God's peace brings a deep, underlying assurance, no matter what circumstances I faced. Fears and doubts were there on the surface, but I could choose to resist them, believe God's promises, and receive his peace. Only his peace could give me the confidence to move ahead in obeying God's plan for me—to go to Thailand.

Chapter Four

STRATEGIC REDIRECTION

As I prepared to go to Thailand, God gave me an exciting verse:

See, I am sending an angel before you to protect you on your journey and lead you safely to the place I have prepared for you.
Exodus 23:20

This was all the confirmation I needed that he was leading me to serve in the Christian hospital in the centre of Thailand. On top of that, as a New Zealand-registered nurse and midwife, Manorom Hospital was clearly a place where God could use my skills. I was encouraged all along to hear that the hospital staff were praying for more nurses to come.

My term of service began with a three-month orientation course in Singapore. And it was there, in my very first week in Singapore, that my confidence was shattered by the devastating news that the Thai government had changed their regulations. Expats were no longer eligible to sit the nursing registration examination. I felt gutted! Having worked and prayed toward this for most of my life, I couldn't believe the door was being shut in my face.

It was time to lean on the promise God had given me. He had said he would send an angel before me to get me to the place he had prepared. And so, I would carry on towards Manorom Hospital with bold confidence. Hadn't his word confirmed it? The leadership of OMF assured me that with the door shut so suddenly to nursing, I could return home if I wanted to. But I was so convinced God's promise meant Manorom that there was no way I was going to turn back. I really believed that God would work in the situation and that the government would change its policy for me so that I could sit the nurses' examination. And so, after my orientation time in Singapore, I moved on to the next stage of my preparation—a year of language school in Bangkok.

Finally, I was in Thailand! I'd arrived at the place God had prepared for my life's ministry. To my surprise, I found things quite the opposite to what I had feared. Thai food wasn't scarily spicy; it was delicious. The temperature was steady for most of the year; it was actually a relief to not have to worry about extra layers of clothes in case of a change of weather as we did in New Zealand. In fact, it was only unbearably hot for two months of the year when temperatures soared during the day and didn't cool down much at night. During those months, I slept under a mosquito net (which had the added bonus of protecting me from the creepy crawlies that fell off the ceiling) with a fan to circulate the air. If it was too hot for sleep, I just got up and had a cold shower, and didn't bother towelling down.

I quickly fell in love with the Thai people. They were friendly, generous and warm, and they prioritised relationships. I learned to appreciate their values, especially the commitment to doing whatever was needed to maintain harmony. They often agreed to things to keep the hearer happy, even if it was not what they really thought.

I found the Thai language much easier to learn than French. I had failed in French in school, which indicated to me I couldn't learn languages. But in Thailand the whole learning system was so different. We were only taught in English for the first month. After that all the lessons were delivered in Thai. By using it daily the vocabulary soon made sense, although I did struggle for the first six months to be able to hear and differentiate the five tones. The way I could butcher a Thai word to give it five different meanings gave the teachers plenty to despair over, along with some laughs.

My first year in Thailand felt like a honeymoon! I was exactly in the place that God had led me to, and he had overcome all my fears. To add to my joy, my Thai language teacher expressed an interest in learning about the gospel. She conversed quite comfortably in English, and so, for three months we studied John's gospel together as she learnt all about Christ and his sacrifice. *Would she like to give her life to Christ?* I asked. "Yes!" she replied enthusiastically. But three days later she was not so sure. "These have been the worst three days in my life," she said. "I've had a terrible headache ever since I received Christ." I was upset. What had gone wrong? Why wasn't she filled with love and joy and peace? What had I done?

As I asked the Lord about this, he revealed some things she

needed to confess and renounce. I asked if she was willing to do that and she said she was, but the next day she didn't turn up at the language school. Someone said they'd seen her leave, carrying a bag. I was very confused. Later we found out where she was, and went to visit her. We had a polite conversation, although she never revealed what she really thought and she never came back to teach. That was my first introduction to the struggle that goes on for a soul who comes to Christ from a totally different background. Nevertheless, I claimed God's promise for her:

I am certain that God, who began the good work within you, will continue his work until it is finally finished on the day when Christ Jesus returns.
Philippians 1:6

This promise encouraged me to be more patient, allowing the Holy Spirit in his own time to reveal to people what they need to deal with.

* * *

With my year of intensive language-learning completed, I was sent to the historical city of Lopburi, about two hours south of Manorom Hospital. There I would continue studying the language while living with four nurses who travelled a hazardous circuit by motorbike to conduct clinics for leprosy sufferers. Leprosy was prevalent and feared at the time; in fact, it was a major part of the reason Manorom Hospital had been founded. These nurses travelled miles over rough roads to care for their clients all day in a *sala* (a shelter with a roof but no walls). Arriving home weary and hungry, they were ready to eat by five o'clock in the evening. But not me. After a day of language study, I was keen to get out and meet with the Thai as they socialised in front of their homes in the cool of early evening. That was when people welcomed visitors. For me, it became a source of frustration to have to be home for the five p.m. meal each day.

Along with language learning, I continued to study for the nursing registration examination, which was all in Thai. To my shock, however, the government did not change their policy, and I was never able to sit the examination. As a result, I went through a time of intense grief. How could I give up the career I loved so much and that so fulfilled my sense of mission? I was profoundly disappointed. I felt as if God had let me down and not fulfilled his promise to get me to Manorom Hospital. It took time to understand that God's promises are not limited to one particular place, but to every place he sends us. He never leaves us, but his plans are not necessarily what we assume.

Occasionally I visited my friend Elaine who worked as a nurse at Manorom. It was always a bit of a drama getting there. First I travelled on a crowded local bus to the Asian highway. Then I had to flag down a northbound tour bus travelling at speed. The only problem was that I couldn't speed-read the curly Thai characters on the destination sign. Many times I missed the bus and had to wait for the next one. So, it was often a tiring journey to actually get to the hospital.

I usually found Elaine busy in the labour ward. On one particular visit, I discovered that there were four women in labour at once. I was really keen to help as they were short-staffed with only one midwife. But I knew I was not legally allowed. Going back outside to hide my distress, I silently cried out to God, "Why won't you let me be a midwife when you can see they are so desperate for someone to help?" God replied very clearly to me that day saying, "What is more important—to be a physical or a spiritual midwife?" I answered, "Well, Lord, you will have to show me the way forward, because I have only seen one person—my language teacher—interested in the gospel in the whole nineteen months I have been here in Thailand!"

But within five minutes of returning from that visit to Manorom, I had a visitor, a young man who asked politely, "Can you tell me how to become a Christian, please?" God was answering my prayer! Over that next year, twelve young adults believed. Four of them later became pastors. God had launched me into a new and thrilling midwifery career!

Chapter Five

Spiritual awakening

To mark the new direction in my ministry, I left the leprosy nursing team and moved in with a fellow Kiwi at the student drop-in centre in Lopburi. Barbara Irwin was an amazing example of faithfulness in following up acquaintances and studying the Bible with young Christians. She ran an open home where students could drop in at any time. And they did! They came and played games or just generally hung out with us and we enjoyed many casual moments sharing the gospel. However, in spite of my enthusiasm, I found the pace exhausting. My language was still limited and I needed to withdraw occasionally to top up on both vocabulary and energy as people came constantly to be set free from evil spirits or drug addiction.

The father of one very new believer was a powerful spirit medium who quickly mustered up fellow mediums to help force his son to return to the spirits. Although we prayed, the boy gradually stopped coming. It was so discouraging, not being sure of how to take authority over the spirit realm and display God's victory. Help came, though, when Pansee, my

Thai language teacher, offered to teach me how to preach! She knew little of the Bible, but as a new believer she was intensely aware of the spiritual realm. She had seen two large snakes slithering from her bedroom and out the door of her house. With Jesus in her life such spirits were unable to stay. She knew that Jesus was real because he was the only divine being she had ever seen during meditation who smiled; all the rest had looked hostile.

I taught her from Revelation chapter twelve, about God's victory over the dragon. This was nothing like the assurance of salvation I would have taught a new Christian in New Zealand! And she taught me. Pansee received the baptism of the Holy Spirit at her conversion and had begun to speak in tongues. We started every lesson with prayer, and she always prayed in tongues. Pansee insisted that having spent many hours in Buddhist meditation, she found this the best way to break through the spiritual barrier and into God's presence. Soon, I too began to sense the presence of God in a way I had never experienced before. Pansee suggested that we would make a good pair because I knew the scriptures and she knew the Holy Spirit!

But constantly seeing first-hand the power of the enemy soon led me to begin doubting the power of God. I had never seen his power on full display; my friends, on the other hand, shared an inexhaustible stream of occultic, melodramatic stories of spirits who seemed so skilled in healing, fertility, or giving material blessings.

One girl I heard of had run away from home to become a Buddhist nun. When it came time to shave her hair, however, she fled and jumped on a bus which happened to be heading to Lopburi. *What should she do?* Someone on the bus told her to visit the missionaries as they would help her. She stayed for a few weeks and heard about Jesus for the first time. But she couldn't become a Christian, she said, because her only friend was a spirit who came and played with her and pushed her toy car around the room. I could hardly believe my ears.

Clearly, I needed God the Holy Spirit to empower me if I was to function in this environment where the demonic manifested wherever we went. I felt fearful and unprotected in this new region. Yet I was determined to break through the satanic barriers we encountered. When two missionaries prayed that I would receive the baptism of the Holy Spirit, I initially received a few words of a new language, but I didn't feel anything, so I doubted if anything had happened! That's when I began praying for a mentor. Soon, God brought another Manorom Hospital nurse, Maj-Lis, into my life. She was a Pentecostal missionary from Sweden, and she was a great help. Through her, God empowered me to pray confidently in the power of the Holy Spirit.

Returning to New Zealand after my first four-year term was a mixed blessing. God used many people to provide insight into what had happened to me, and how the power of the Holy Spirit can be shown in so many different ways. It was amazing! Like a jigsaw, God was putting pieces together every place I went.

Lorraine and Allan Scarlet were my mentors, and as lifelong friends and Pentecostal pastors, they understood me. I loved their gentle approach. They accepted where I was in my journey and never pushed anything onto me. They demonstrated the absolute necessity of ministering in the Spirit through love, whatever the gift.

Before returning to Thailand, I spent a few days in prayer and fasting to seek God for direction. When he led me to Isaiah 61, I knew that this was to be the basis of my future ministry, just as it was for Jesus (see Luke 4), although I had no idea how it would work out in reality:

> *The mighty Spirit of Lord Yahweh is wrapped around me because Yahweh has anointed me, as a messenger to preach good news to the poor. He sent me to heal the wounds of the broken-hearted, to tell captives, "You are free", and to tell prisoners, "Be free from your darkness." I am sent to announce a new season of Yahweh's grace and a time of God's recompense on his enemies, to comfort all who are in sorrow, to strengthen those crushed by despair who mourn in Zion—to give them a beautiful bouquet in the place of ashes, the oil of bliss instead of tears, and the mantle of joyous praise instead of the spirit of heaviness. Because of this, they will be known as Mighty Oaks of Righteousness, planted by Yahweh as a living display of his glory.*
> Isaiah 61:1-3 TPT

On my return to Thailand, I asked to live with a Thai family for two months in order to be immersed in Thai culture. Pansee, my language teacher, invited me to stay with her. She happily added me to the family of five teenagers, her elderly parents and two nieces! They lived in a traditional house on stilts and were quite poor, having no regular income apart from occasional language teaching for missionaries. I insisted on living as they lived, with no favours. That meant only two meals a day, consisting mainly of rice and vegetables with chilli and fish sauce for flavour. Occasionally they added some chicken or tiny fish from the paddy fields.

This was an amazing experience. I shared a double mattress with Pansee and her oldest daughter. Pansee didn't seem to need much sleep, and regularly chatted until it was nearly midnight. Then at four thirty in the morning she would wake me by singing worship songs, and we would spend time with the Lord together. What a joy to be with someone so hungry to grow in God! Next came the cold 'shower' at dawn, when we wrapped a *pha* (sarong) around us and dipped cold water out of an enormous water pot. The freezing waterfall stimulated many colourful Thai expressions! Usually, I skimped on the water and waited until the afternoon warmth for a more pleasant experience.

Pansee was a real intercessor and we prayed regularly for all her children and family who were not yet believers. Gradually over the years each of her children became Christians. She had an amazing degree of faith in God's word and firmly believed he would provide for all their needs. Together we prayed for the city to be set free from its pervasive and blatant spirit of oppression, putting on the armour of God first, as we often experienced the backlash of the enemy.

I left Pansee's home after two months to set up a student hostel where young women could be discipled and tutored. Many girls in the region had to leave school prematurely in order to support their families, but they continued to study at night. Gop was a fourteen-year-old girl who asked if I could take her in. With her mother in Hong Kong and an absentee father, she was desperately lonely. Out of compassion, I agreed. She came to church with us but suffered with migraines after each service. One day I found her rolled up in a foetal position, uncommunicative. Urgently, I asked the Lord what was going on. She was wearing a jade monkey amulet, and I wondered if this had anything to do with what was happening. I had no idea if amulets had power or not! So, I asked her if I could take it for a few days and ask God to show me.

That night, Gop had a dream. She saw herself dressed in the armour of God; she held a huge hammer in her hand and was bashing the amulet with it! The following morning, she asked me to give the amulet back, then proceeded to smash it to pieces, just as she had in her dream! From that point on, her migraines disappeared. Of course, this was all new territory for me. How I appreciated Pansee's support with such experiences.

Two of the hostel students became lifelong friends. Pon was an eighteen-year-old who had lived with Barbara and been discipled by her for a while. Pon sold food in the day market and attended classes at night to finish her first year of high school. She was a very sad and withdrawn young woman who had been rejected by her dysfunctional family. But oh, her hunger for God! I longed to encourage her in her spiritual growth. But when she left to live with her sister after four months, I felt such a failure. I had not been able to get close enough to help her resolve her deep-set emotional needs, and I was uncertain of where those needs were coming from. So I specifically handed her over to God, asking him to please keep his hand on her. Incredibly, this prayer was answered—Pon studied at a Bible College and served as a valued teacher at OMF's language school. Later, God led her to start a new church in Lopburi—there, about two hundred people came to the Lord and were nurtured, some of whom were sent out into fulltime ministry.

Laiet was another young woman who came to the hostel. She worked as a seamstress during the day and studied in the evenings. Like Pon, she had a difficult childhood, having been raised by her alcoholic father after her mother died of tuberculosis. Laiet heard the gospel at Manorom Hospital while her mother was a patient. One day her father was performing a ceremony to worship the spirits. When she refused to join in, he told her to leave the house. If she wanted to follow Christ, he said, then Christ would have to care for her. Laiet packed a small bag and fled to the next town, where she lived with Barbara for a year.

Laiet was hungry to grow in her knowledge of God. One day I asked if she wanted to be baptised with the Holy Spirit. However, while I was praying for her, an evil spirit manifested! I was shocked and greatly disturbed. I hadn't realised that her father had offered her to the spirits as a child.

My first reaction was that I had done something wrong. I visited a well-known Thai Pentecostal pastor in Bangkok and explained the situation. "Your team doesn't work routinely in the gifts of the Spirit so you don't know how to respond quickly, using the gifts," he said. "Tell her to read God's Word and the Holy Spirit will lead her." I went home and shared this with Laiet. From that point on, God then began to give her dreams and prophecies. When she shared them with me, I was amazed at their accuracy. I had learnt an important lesson—to check the background of new believers and make sure they renounced any prior involvement with spirits.

Laiet went on to attend Bible College for three years. There she met Boonrod whom she later married. Together they engaged in church planting in a number of cities, including Bannokkamin, the home of Bangkok's 'street boys'. Laiet and I maintained our friendship over the years, and I was often awestruck at what God revealed to her. She loved spending as much time with him as she could, even if it was in the middle of the night.

In 2016 Laiet was diagnosed with lung cancer and told she had only a few months to live. To the astonishment of the doctors, God allowed her another three years and gave her strength to travel the four-hour round trip to Suphanburi, where she and Boonrod planted yet another church. In spite of her increasing frailty, God used Laiet in healing others, and until very near the end she continued to visit and encourage the church cell groups.

I was with her for the last two weeks of her life and once again was awed by her sense of the presence of Jesus. Still, her death was a dilemma for us. We had prayed for her healing, believing God for a miracle. Her daughter asked Jesus why he wasn't healing her and he answered that she had already had three extra years. Only when she saw a vision of her mother walking away hand in hand with Jesus was she able to accept her mother had died.

It was wonderful to see both Pon and Laiet grow into such maturity and fruitful ministry over the years. They enabled many to be set free from the occult, and trained their spiritual children to serve the Lord too. Like them, I determined to focus on bringing the light rather than on fighting the darkness!

Chapter Six

Anchored in God

Before going to Thailand, I had faced the reality that I might remain single. I knew that a mission career would limit my options for marriage, but at twenty-seven years of age I was far more focussed on God's call on my life to serve him overseas. Yet I felt the need for a husband to journey with me. "Do I wait for a husband?" I asked God, "or should I just go in obedience to you and believe your promise that you can meet all my needs, physical, spiritual and emotional?" My confidence was in him.

> *I am convinced that my God will fully satisfy every need you have, for I have seen the abundant riches of glory revealed to me through Jesus Christ!*
> *Philippians 4:19 TPT*

That verse helped, but the situation remained a dilemma. I needed a clearer answer from God. That's when he led me to the scripture:

> *My soul, wait silently for God alone, for my expectation is from Him. He only is my rock and my salvation; He is my defense; I shall not be moved.*
> *Psalm 62:5-6 NKJV*

I appreciated that if I anchored my expectation in God, I would never be disappointed, but if marriage was my primary focus, I might very well be disappointed.

I had prayed for quite some time about a friend I admired, asking God that he would express an interest in me. God led me to pray he would be given the right wife for him. However, the day I heard he was dating a close friend my emotions collapsed. The radio was blaring in the background when suddenly a song began to play. I recognised the words from the book of Habakkuk:

> *Even though the fig trees have no blossoms, and there are no grapes on the vines... yet I will rejoice in the Lord! I will be joyful in the God of my salvation!*
> Habakkuk 3:17-18

Yes, I could trust and rejoice in God no matter what! Eventually, it became obvious to me that my friend was indeed the right partner for him, and I gladly blessed their marriage.

But arriving in Thailand and living in a household of single nurses soon jerked my awareness of my single state. I was dismayed to discover that my room had a double bed! In the 1980's it was usual for a single man or woman to have a single bed. Neither my linen nor my thoughts coped with the situation. *Why do I get the double bed? Why is there still no husband?*

Parted from my family and friends, I began to ache for physical contact. Even nursing would have been fulfilling. But suddenly I was immersed in an expat culture where touch was off-limits. Fellow New Zealanders, who hugged me back home, didn't touch me in Thailand out of respect for protocol.

I had read that humans need ten hugs per day to survive. I shared this with God. "I don't know how I'm going to survive. If you can't meet my emotional needs I'm not *going* to survive!" Figuring the answer must have something to do with the Holy Spirit, I set out to get to know him better.

Shortly after, I was invited to spend a weekend with a German family with two little girls, aged three and five. These youngsters spent the weekend jumping all over me on the couch. I laughed to myself as I realised what God was doing, giving me the hands-on happiness I ached for.

God also gave me wonderful opportunities to connect with people on my visits back to New Zealand. I once attended a missionary retreat for singles run by a couple called John and Agnes Sturt. John was a medical doctor, counsellor and spiritual director. He discussed singleness, and also named touch as a basic need for every human being. He had each of us stand in a circle and give the shoulders of the person in front a shoulder massage. This felt so intrusive to me at the time! When he gave me a copy of his book *Created for Intimacy*, I was shocked to read that every person, single or married, needs to have an intimate relationship with at least one other person, to allow another person to see into your heart and to experience mutual acceptance. When I asked him why this was so important, John Sturt replied that we must learn to have mature relationships where we actually work through issues between each other, and that sharing at a spiritual level would enable this to happen more easily.

What a recipe for healthy, happy living! Without doubt, my sense of singleness had made me awkward in developing give-and-take relationships with married team members. I was particularly conscious of avoiding any offense in relating to men. I felt the odd one out, little appreciating that loneliness affects all members of missionary teams whether single or married. Often a wife is home alone for days, even nights, on end, unable to engage in the active ministry she once longed passionately for. She may feel isolated or side-lined even while busy with young children . . . or aching for them far away at boarding school. One mother told me that crises escalated whenever her husband was away. Her reason for clinging in tears to the Lord was different but just as valid as mine.

In the earlier years, I was passionate to see the Thai coming to Christ and was willing to make any sacrifice in my own personal life to see this happen. As a result, I failed to appreciate the stresses that wives were facing, and they often failed to understand the stresses of singleness. Occasionally, however, it was our theological stance that added complication to relationships. Over the space of ten years, I was privileged to lead three different teams. As a matriarchal society, Thailand gives status to professional women, single or married, and I was comfortable in that sphere. However, the majority of couples in my care came from environments where it was less acceptable for women to be in leadership. When our expat team met for business, we were inclined to revert and be inhibited by our cultural norms. They often appeared to be unresponsive and I felt totally frustrated, in the wrong, and alone. Why didn't all the team members speak up at meetings? It wasn't until later that I realised how difficult it was for those couples to accept my leadership because of a different theological view regarding women! Thankfully, God gave me caring leaders who were available to help me see the situation from all sides and work through the struggles I was facing. I'm grateful too, for the God-given ability to focus on one day at a time and find him sufficient. I just don't have the right to demand that satisfaction will be through one particular person or in one specific way.

Throughout my years in Thailand, my mum and dad were great encouragers with their regular writing, but our letters took three weeks to round off even one conversation. Costly phone calls were restricted to once a year for birthdays, or for emergencies. They also necessitated a trip to the post office or 'phone shop' with faint hope of a clear connection.

After our first year in Thailand, OMF workers qualified for a break at the mission holiday home in Hua Hin. What joy! Now we could look forward to a seaside holiday for two weeks every six months with everything done for us, from meals to laundry. The chores of daily living in Thailand were exhausting, and we often spent the first week just sleeping and relaxing.

But I found that by the second week, my holiday deteriorated. Couples did their thing, sometimes inviting me to join them. But with so much time to compare, I began to feel condemned, to suspect I wasn't acceptable to God. Not realising that childhood abuse can leave a false sense of shame, I often ended up feeling depressed instead of refreshed. Would I ever really rest and be at peace?

The library proved a mixed blessing. I launched into reading the shelf of romantic novels but soon realised this wasn't helpful for me. It stirred up so many longings that I had to stop. Then I found an amazing commentary on the Song of Solomon, written by Hudson Taylor, the founder of OMF. I was stunned to read that the Song of Solomon was about having a personal love relationship with Christ. His insights absorbed me. I still have the Bible where I crammed all my notes into the margins. I jotted down terms of endearment into my journal and made them personal. I determined to believe that this was how Christ saw me. The words gave me such hope that God loved me personally and called me his own! He didn't see any blemish in me, just perfection. It was mind blowing!

> *My darling, you are so lovely! You are beauty itself to me.*
> *Your passionate eyes are like gentle doves.*
> *Song of Songs 1:15 TPT*

> *Yes, you are my darling companion. You stand out from all the rest. For though the thorns surround you, you remain as pure as a lily.*
> *Song of Songs 2:2 TPT*

> *Every part of you is so beautiful, my darling. Perfect is your beauty, without flaw within.*
> *Song of Songs 4:7 TPT*

My singleness wasn't a constant struggle. At times I felt totally fulfilled knowing that God loved me and chose me to share his love with others. But there were other times, when I lived alone or saw little happen in the work, that I found his assurances hard to believe. The enemy would close in to accuse and condemn me, "You're not good enough for God, you're not doing enough, you're a failure." Darting thoughts stabbed my mind. It was like a default setting in my brain from childhood. Self-criticism and condemnation seemed poised to pop up from the moment I woke up till I went to bed. I had to reset; to choose deliberately to believe what God said about me through his promises; to dismiss, my own condemning thoughts.

In those days we were not given a choice about who we lived or worked with. We were simply assigned to live with another single. Staffing the teams was always tight and singles were pulled in to plug the gaps. It was also considered unhealthy for us singles to stay in the same team for more than three or four years in case we became co-dependent. As a result, we had little continuity in relationships and faced the constant, daunting prospect of having to adjust to new fellow workers every term of service. It gobbled up enormous energy to establish each new relationship and there never seemed to be any sense of unconditional love. Thankfully, OMF now gives single workers the choice to live alone or to choose a mutual companion, and there is no requirement to change living arrangements at the end of each ministry assignment.

I was often envious of the expat families. It seemed they had a valid excuse to take time out, a God-given, built-in way to relax. Children were also amazing little 'ice-breakers', casually opening the way into the hearts of others. People didn't seem as keen to know their solo neighbour after hours. But while these dynamics were real, God was about to show me something deeper.

Isaiah 54:4-5 (TPT) reads:

> *Do not fear, for your shame is no more. Do not be embarrassed for you will not be disgraced. You will forget the inadequacy you felt in your youth and will no longer remember the shame of your widowhood. For your Maker is your husband.*

This came as such a wonderful promise to me because I had no idea how to get over the shame of my youth. Eventually I came to realise that the condemning voice churning my emotions was not God speaking to me. It was the voice of a false identity I had adopted in childhood. Falsehood was my default position! It has been a life-long struggle to believe what God says about me and not what seems normal for me to feel and think. Now, whether it's day or night, I pour out my thoughts and prayers, knowing that God is always with me as companion and husband.

As I look back, I can see that God has regularly surprised me by bringing along a companion for part of the journey. Airini my sister-in-law, came for two months to help teach at the English school before we holidayed together. What a gift it was to have her wise support and fresh perspective on my situation. Of course, before long, those of us 'on the field' who loved to use leisure time to pray, booked holidays together. We would spend a few hours each day in praise and worship, praying for breakthrough in Thailand. Those times were like heaven on earth. And the company has not always been in person—I have had numerous prayer companions who are like unsung heroes, of inestimable value.

One of the advantages of being single in Thailand was being free to do what I liked without always deferring to someone else. Some of my married friends seemed hobbled when it came to quick decision-making! A down-side was that when no one was around for socialising, I tended to just keep working.

Inviting Thai young women to live with me made a huge difference. It enriched my understanding of the Thai language and allowed my existing friendships to deepen. The students gave me valuable insights into how their culture and society worked. They also gave me greater awareness of myself. I remember soon after opening the hostel I was coming downstairs one morning to go to the bathroom when I noticed my friends looking anxious. "Why are you angry?" they asked. "You stomped down the stairs!" "I'm not angry," I replied with a laugh, "I'm just in a hurry to go to the loo!" I was learning that body language often gets interpreted differently in different cultures!

Because I was single, I had hours to listen to my Thai friends, many of whom I had known since their teenage years. I learned of the deep pains they experienced both in childhood and throughout life. We developed precious heart relationships and they became substitute family. But having poured my heart into student ministry for more than a decade, I sensed the Lord was about to shift my focus.

Chapter Seven

Facing Oppression

Sitting down with Ian Roberts, my OMF leader, I explained that I was sensing it was time to begin working with adults rather than students. What a surprise when he responded by asking if I would consider starting a church in a provincial town that had never had a Christian place of worship! The Phrabaht (meaning 'Buddha's footprint') district was unfamiliar to me, and I had no idea how to go about starting a new church. Ian suggested that I start with two women who had recently come to Christ. Both were in their sixties, and we referred to them as 'aunties.' Aunty Sombon and Aunty Jian had independently travelled forty-five minutes by bus to find a church in Lopburi, the provincial capital, but had not met each other. *Why not visit these two ladies in Phrabaht, and start a home fellowship with them and their friends?* So, I got in touch and asked if they would help me with some house-hunting.

What a worthwhile introduction that proved to be! The night before I arrived, Aunty Sombon had a dream. In her dream, an old man with a rod came and held it over Phrabaht. She also saw many stars falling. Aunty Sombon believed that God was giving us his authority and that we would see God open up the way, like he had the Red Sea, for many to come to Christ. Right from the outset, God gave her the gift of intercession!

We found a small house quite close to the market and arranged for me to move in the following week. It was dark and lacked a kitchen, so everything was done on the open back porch—food preparation, dish washing, laundry. Inside was a small gas stove and a fridge.

It took four months for me to cajole these two ladies to meet together. Whenever I went to their houses individually to teach the Bible they were delighted. But if I suggested that the three of us study together, they just weren't interested. Buddhists are used to individual worship and don't understand Christian fellowship. It was after they were baptised, that everything changed. Aunty Sombon and Aunty Jian became bolder to witness and more willing to meet together on Sundays. Even so, it was tough going. One day as we sat there struggling to sing, I despaired. How could God ever make a church out of us three? None of us could hold a tune and they didn't know any Christian songs. But believe me, God is a God who fulfils his promises! Matthew 16:18 reminds us that God will build his church, and the gates of hell will not prevail against it. And that's exactly what he did.

Aunty Jian began to witness as she sold her homemade Thai salads. The boxing ring was a routine sales stop. But one burly boxer never paid up. When she suggested he did, he pulled a gun on her and demanded she keep giving him food regardless. Boldly she answered, "Shoot me if you like! I believe in Jesus and I know I'm going to heaven." At that he dropped the gun and knelt down in penitence. Aunty Jian was totally shocked. From then on, he paid for his takeaways.

Her other source of income was massage. She chatted throughout the session, inviting her clients to come along to church and then to stay for lunch together afterwards. Some of her friends were spirit mediums. When they came and ate the food that was blessed, the spirits in them reacted by beating them up, leaving bruises all over their bodies. "Aunty Jian, we can't come again!" they said. I was in awe that simply 'saying grace' for our food thwart the spirits so powerfully!

After a while a new fellow worker from a very different cultural background arrived and we agreed to share my home for a month to see how things worked out. She was used to working independently, and though I didn't know it, so was I! This made us both very stressed and after a few months our regional leader moved her to another city.

After she left, I experienced deep spiritual oppression. The enemy accused and condemned me. "If you can't get on with a fellow worker how will God ever use you to plant a church?" I totally fell for this seemingly accurate assessment. For the next nine months I woke feeling paralysed, unable to get out of bed each morning until I had listened to worship music and spent time with God receiving his strength. I remember reading a book called *Mountain Rain*. This was the biography of James O. Fraser, an OMF missionary to tribal people in China. In it, the author shared how he'd come under intense oppression when he first preached to the Lisu people in China, to the point where he couldn't get out of bed. He said he felt as if the enemy came over him like an insidious gas vapour, like a wet blanket, paralysing and asphyxiating him. I realised I was experiencing a typical attack of the enemy after going into a new area. Being on my own fed my vulnerability. The only way to overcome it was to overcome the enemy by the blood of the Lamb and the word of my testimony (Revelation 12:11). Every day I would say, "I believe I am covered by the blood of the Lamb. I am going out into the market to look for someone with whom to share the gospel. Please put your words into my mouth." Then I would find someone, get chatting, and return home with a renewed sense of victory and encouragement. God was enabling me to overcome the enemy on a day-by-day basis.

One of my neighbours in Phrabaht was a quadriplegic. She lay on her front porch with little social interaction, so I'd call in. One day as I shared about Jesus, I asked if she believed in him. Her eyes teared up and she agreed to be led in a prayer to accept him as her saviour. Another time I asked if she would like me to pray for her to go to heaven and be released from constant agony. Ten days later she developed a fever and went to be with the Lord. I could imagine her walking with him, free at last from pain and completely whole. For me it was a sign that God's Spirit was starting to move, even though this precious lady didn't 'count' for local church growth!

***

From the day I arrived in Phrabaht, I had prayed that God would send me a 'Rahab'—someone who would give me a way in to the community. Not long after, I met a Christian nurse's aide working at the local hospital. She took me to meet her sister and brother-in-law during their lunch break. Unbeknown to me her brother-in-law was a practising spirit medium. I had brought with me a poster to share the good news of Jesus. One of the pictures on the poster portrayed a black heart with green demons in residence. This picture really convicted him and suddenly he wanted to be free. That desire triggered such turmoil in his heart, and at times the spirit completely took over. A few months later, he was overcome by God's love as he watched a Christmas movie with us. He longed to receive Jesus but said he would wait until New Year. I warned him it might not be safe to wait, especially with the overwhelming spiritual pressures of the New Year ceremonies. "The spirit in you will not be happy. Don't leave it too long," I said.

Four days later, God spoke to me that he was going to give victory to this young man over the spirits. That evening he arrived with his wife on the back of his motorbike. "We *both* want to give our lives to Jesus!" he said. There and then I led them in a prayer to receive Christ, and the following day I asked my team leader to send a Thai pastor to help them be set completely free.

Having been thrown into spiritual warfare essentially on my own, I asked God to send me an experienced intercessor. "I can't cope alone," I prayed. "I need someone who knows how to pray to come and stand with me in praying for breakthrough." The very next week I received a letter from a friend at Manorom Hospital asking if I would like to have an intercessor from England visit me for three days while she took a break from her own short-term mission trip. I jumped at the opportunity and thanked God for this favour!

Truda was a seventy-year-old woman with a passion for missions. After one hour of praying for Phrabaht she declared we were not getting anywhere sitting down; we needed to march around the city and proclaim God's victory. I had read about this approach but had never done it so I was glad for her to take the lead. We walked around the hospital and all the major buildings in the city proclaiming Christ's Lordship. It was exhilarating to actually do something significant in the spiritual realm.

That night, I dreamed that Buddha was angry with me. The next morning as Truda was praying, I saw the same Buddha again. Truda said to me, "God has sent you into this city to take authority over it. You need to proclaim God's victory." I felt so condemned and weak that I didn't want to do it, but she encouraged me to exercise the authority God had given me. As I took authority, she saw a vision of a row of spirits being taken captive and another row of townspeople being released from captivity. She said emphatically, "That's what is going to happen here."

The third morning, we'd just sat down to breakfast when the young man so recently freed from spirit control arrived on his motorbike with his sister onboard. God had woken her up at four a.m. and told her to get a ride on a truck heading to the market. She called her brother to ask if he could take her to the missionaries he'd told her about? She hoped we could free her from the torment of a resident spirit. She'd invited it in, hoping for good luck. Instead, it punished her when she didn't do what it told her. She looked petrified while we explained the gospel to her. But she listened and was adamant that she wanted to receive Jesus. As we prayed for her to trust in Jesus and his truth, we also commanded the resident spirit to leave, and prayed for her to be filled with the Holy Spirit.

The day after Truda left, I went to visit this new believer to find out how she was. She replied, "In my dream last night, my old spirit guide was shot dead. While I was crying, a new man came to me dressed in white and he said to me, 'You will find out about me in the book!'"

The book! Handing her a Bible I said, "Oh, that's the Holy Spirit of Jesus, and I've just come to introduce you to him." She was delighted as we studied God's Word and began to understand that the Holy Spirit had taken up residence in her already, that he promised never to leave her, and to guide her into all truth. She was hungry to learn more about God and to remove all the paraphernalia used in her occultic rituals. She went on to tell me that she had endured three operations to remove kidney stones. Each time, the stones were visible on x-ray, but whenever the surgeons operated, they were just not there. She said that if she had known Jesus earlier, she would not have gone through all that agony.

From then on, many friends, neighbours and relatives of the new believers became curious to learn about Jesus. But by now Truda had returned to Manorom, and I ached even more for a fellow overcomer. As the attacks of oppression and condemnation intensified, I wasn't sure that I was going to survive emotionally.

One day soon after, I went to the post office and discovered a letter from Mum. She was no artist, but she'd drawn a God-inspired picture of someone hanging on a noose with hills behind. I was so surprised to see this because it looked just like the hills of Phrabaht and this was exactly how I felt. But what delighted me most was that the noose was broken at the front. It gave me such hope. Now I knew that I was going to survive!

I was so grateful for the prayers of God's people. I had discovered, like so many other missionaries, that it was absolutely essential to have prayer partners upholding our hands when we were in the front line of battle. No wonder it was a prerequisite in our mission agency to build prayer support teams who committed to pray daily for us.

I had focussed on praying for the new believers. Having read about a missionary who led tribal people to the Lord then fasted seven days for each one to make sure that they were completely set free, I decided to follow his example. But when more and more folk believed, I had to admit failure. "Lord, I don't seem to have many days left to eat in a month! I think I just need to fast one day a week if that's okay."

Increasingly, I also realised I needed to safeguard myself in this new province. Since moving to Phrabaht, I had asked God for angels to surround the house and protect me. One morning I knew that prayer had been effective when I woke to discover that the door and a window had been forced open. Strangely, however, my motorbike and computer were still there. In fact, nothing was missing! I called the owner who lived next door who confirmed the break-in. The words of

Psalm 91 came to mind, and instinctively I knew the burglars had been confronted by an angel!

> *When we live our lives within the shadow of God Most High, our secret hiding place, we will always be shielded from harm. How then could evil prevail against us or disease infect us? God sends angels with special orders to protect you wherever you go, defending you from all harm.*
> *Psalm 91:9-11 TPT*

Even so, I knew I couldn't go it alone for much longer.

Chapter Eight

Walking in Authority

I had been in Phrabaht for eight months when God brought a woman by the name of Arlene Sorensen to serve alongside me in the work. What a delight she was! Just a few days after her arrival, I wrote in my diary:

> *"Arlene is encouraging, accepting, sympathetic, makes me want to weep because of the love I sense instead of condemnation. She frees me to be myself and gives me confidence in ministry. We are both determined to support one another in ministry and be of one heart and mind."*

Arlene had such a gentle and compassionate spirit, and was genuinely interested in people. Together we laughed through the initial culture shock. Life in this dusty Thai town was far removed from the idyllic setting of her rural American upbringing! But the number one thing that bound us together was our desire to seek God in prayer regularly and to remain united in support of each other. Friday mornings were set aside for prayer and were always a highlight.

On the other days of the week, Arlene concentrated on language study in the mornings so that we could go out together in the afternoons and often into the evening when people were home from work. We both loved getting on the motorbike, loaded with our pictorial posters and an old slide projector. We found that a visual presentation of the life of Jesus stimulated valuable discussion and led to whole families being impacted. Occasionally the box of slides would spill out over the floor and everyone would pitch in enthusiastically to get them back in order again. It was a fun way to 'break the ice' in a new environment.

God had given me a wonderful promise for the city of Prabaht—one that indicated not only the level of breakthrough we should expect, but also the darkness and oppression we would face:

> *Darkness as black as night covers all the nations of the earth, but the glory of the Lord rises to appear over you. All nations will come to your light; mighty kings will come to see your radiance.*
> Isaiah 60:2-3

We enjoyed seeing light come to our city as God answered our earnest prayers. Still, the darkness was ever-present, and we faced repeated spiritual attack. Needing God's constant wisdom, protection and direction, we often turned to Psalm twenty-seven as we claimed God's promises together:

> *The Lord is my light and my salvation—whom shall I fear? The Lord is the stronghold of my life—of whom shall I be*

afraid? When the wicked advance against me to devour me, it is my enemies and my foes who will stumble and fall. Though an army besiege me, my heart will not fear; though war break out against me, even then will I be confident.
Psalm 27:1-3 NIV

Our confidence was especially needed the day we went to visit a new believer by the name of Mr Pon. We had set out on our motorbike, and were happily making our way down the muddy road towards his farmhouse when the motorbike skipped out from under us and we both tumbled off. Picking ourselves up, we got back on the bike, but we arrived filthy, shaken, and unsure about how we would be received. As it turned out, our mishap immediately endeared us to our hosts. Mr Pon had a more pressing concern—before coming to Christ he would have asked the spirits to show him the best site to place a well. Now that he was a believer, he wanted us to ask God on his behalf. We prayed, believing that God would reveal it to him. God did so and next time when we visited, the pump was delivering water most efficiently. God was very gracious to these new believers—and gracious to us too, as he turned adversity into advantage.

We found that most of the people who came to Christ experienced symptoms of enemy attack and needed to be set free. Some had high fevers, others experienced headaches and one old man fainted each day while riding his bike. He said, "I can't go to work anymore. Ever since I became a Christian I faint while I'm riding my bike!" Knowing that he needed to be released from spirits, I asked if he had dedicated his house to God. "No!" he replied. "Please come and pray." I felt pretty confident about this and quickly went into action. Afterwards, however, I became very weak. I knew I needed to pause and claim God's protection. It was important that my growing confidence did not deteriorate into relying on my own energy instead of his.

One Sunday a man by the name of Mr Taw walked into our gathering and announced that he wanted to receive Jesus. His daughter had been witnessing to him most effectively. What we didn't know was that he was due to receive the annual visitation of a spirit in his village that day. He'd contrived to escape and receive Jesus instead! But the next Sunday, a young Christian by the name of Somchai came with the news that Mr Taw was lying paralysed in the shape of a cross and could not get up. We went to visit him that afternoon and claimed deliverance. His elderly wife was there too. She was very stooped over, having been gored by a bull. The Buddhist monks refused to stoop so that she could put offerings in their bowls—as a result, she was unable to make 'essential merit.'

We could see that Mr Taw's wife was bowed down, not only physically, but by the fear of an unprotected life. That day, she too decided to give her life to Jesus. When we prayed for her husband to be delivered, unbeknown to us the spirit transferred to the wife and she had the same paralysing symptoms for the next week. But this couple were so committed to the Lord that nothing derailed their faith. Since neither of them could read, we loaned them a cassette player and a selection of Christian teachings. Mr Taw received the gift of intercession, praying with more faith than all the rest of us combined! Though all his friends from the temple deserted him, Mr Taw was delighted with his new friend, Jesus, who answered prayer.

By the end of our first year, many people had shown an interest in the gospel and I was due for a holiday. Pastor Udom Chuduang, a Thai evangelist, and his wife had visited previously and so I asked if they would come and carry on the work for a few weeks while I took a break. Little did I know that during that short time, another forty people would be led to the Lord, despite the fact that many were in varying states of inebriation. Pastor Udom's firm conviction was that you must lead every person to the Lord the first time they heard the gospel. "What if it was their last opportunity?" he said. "What if they went out and got shot?"

His concern was founded on grim personal experience in the 'wild west' of Thailand. He also understood the viciousness of spiritual attack when would-be believers were ambivalent about making a clear decision to accept Christ into their lives. He likened it to being in a spiritual no-man's land between two opposing forces. Below the ethical requirements of Buddhism lay the swirling sphere of power encounters; capricious spirits demanding to be placated. Now they must be defeated by the authority and power of the risen Lord Jesus Christ.

When I returned from holiday, I continued to follow up the new believers, leading 'cell groups' six nights a week. Sadly, three of those who professed to believe had second thoughts once they'd sobered up and went to the temple to have the 'Jesus spirit' chased out of them. Later we learnt that two of those three experienced serious accidents and were killed. We and the new believers were increasingly experiencing God's awesome presence and power.

Through this time, twelve other people began taking hesitant steps towards the Lord. They were dragged from their initial commitment, however, by various fears and by continuing to dabble in spirit rituals as a precaution in case the God we spoke of proved inadequate to protect them. We agonised over the danger of their vacillating—and for good reason. Each of these twelve experienced unnatural deaths; one fell from a coconut tree and another onto concrete; one had a motorbike accident, and others were either shot dead or so overcome by the power of the spirits that they were asphyxiated. In every case, the hospital staff were unable to resuscitate them.

I cried out in fearfulness to God. I told him I didn't feel safe sharing the gospel any more as so many were dying before they fully trusted him. I knew we were totally dependent on him, and when he showed me what was happening, I realised that we needed to pray for protection over those who expressed an interest in following Christ:

> *We have become the unmistakable aroma of the victory of the Anointed One to God—a perfume of life to those being saved and the odour of death to those who are perishing.*
> 2 Corinthians 2:15 TPT

One of those who followed through with their expression of interest in the gospel, was a young woman called Noy. She and her friend, Lek, turned up at our home one day, with Noy determined to become a Christian. After the joy of leading her in prayer, we celebrated with a meal together. But halfway through the meal, Noy jumped up and hurried outside. Hearing the unpleasant sound of vomiting, Arlene offered to go and see how she was while I kept the conversation going inside. The next moment Arlene cried out for help. Hearing the panic in her voice, I ran outside to find Noy lying on the ground as if she were dead. "What happened?" I asked. Arlene explained that she had merely placed a hand on Noy and prayed for her, whereupon the girl had collapsed. Neither of us understood what we were dealing with—there was no sign of vomit on the ground, and when I tried to rouse Noy, she was unresponsive. Together, Arlene and I carried her inside and lay her on the floor.

Was this connected with the prayer Noy had just prayed? Arlene, who had only been in Phrabaht a month by now, was uncomfortable with such spiritual manifestations and stood back, not knowing what to do. I had never seen anything quite like this either, but I knew enough to realise that what we were dealing with was a demonic spirit. Realising that Noy's father was a spirit medium, I asked Lek if this happened very often. She assured us it was a regular occurrence.

Thanks to Pansee, I had enough knowledge of the spiritual realm to know what we needed to do. Following my lead, Arlene and I began singing worship songs, and I began to declare scripture over our young friend about the power of the blood of Christ to set her free. Understanding my spiritual authority, I eventually stood my ground and commanded the spirit to leave Noy alone. When, after two hours, we seemed to have made no progress, I asked Arlene to commit Noy to God in prayer. As she prayed, Noy opened her eyes and said, "What's been happening?"

After we had ministered to Noy, she and her friend stayed in our house overnight. I concluded that she would not be completely set free until we helped her renounce all the occult involvement she had previously been involved with. We had experienced a level of victory, but it was clear we urgently needed help from someone, preferably a Thai, who was familiar with such battles.

The following day I phoned my field leader and explained the situation. It really was getting beyond me and I wasn't sure how to proceed, and Arlene wasn't sure what to make of it all. He told us that a Thai leader was due to visit a nearby town the following week. This man was experienced in deliverance ministry. I should take Noy to see him.

Somsak Choosong was the principal of Phayao Bible College, and his message to Noy was blunt: "You either believe one hundred percent in Jesus or you go crazy with spirit attacks." It seemed extreme to talk this way to a ten-day-old believer, but Somsak understood that because Noy's father had been a pedlar of the occult, she was particularly sensitive and vulnerable to attack. Pastor Somsak explained that spiritual attacks often presented as a sharp pain in the head, stomach or heart. A believer should renounce the attacker for themselves in the name of Jesus, he said, and command it to go. I realised then that I had been the victim of an aching shoulder since laying hands on Noy the previous week, so I commanded the pain to leave even as he was speaking and was immediately set free. From that point on, I was able to teach the new believers how to renounce the enemy when he attacked using pains, fainting, or any other aberrations.

So humble yourselves before God. Resist the devil, and he will flee from you. Come close to God, and God will come close to you.
James 4:7-8

The need to recognise and resist the devil became particularly urgent one day when, during a tropical downpour, Arlene and I were jerked awake at midnight by loud banging at the door. Noy and Lek were standing in the teeming rain calling my name. "Please come and help us!" pleaded Noy, "my father's house is flooding!" My initial reaction was to say, "no way," but I knew that as 'a good Christian' we should be willing to help! As we hurried to dress, they added, "and please bring your camera!"

Why a camera at midnight? I wondered. It all seemed very strange. When we arrived at their house, it was completely flooded with water. The girls asked me to take some photos of the mess but assured me they didn't want any other help. In fact, they told us we could go home again.

A few days later I took them the photos. Until the night of the flood I had avoided visiting Noy in her home because I was apprehensive about meeting Noy's father who was a spirit medium. When I arrived at the house, I was led into the main living area. There, to my horror, Noy's father was consulting the spirits on behalf of a woman. Even though I was seated at the other end of the room, I felt his eyes boring right through me. In a monotone he ordered, "Get her a coffee." I didn't like coffee, yet I knew it was polite to accept whatever was offered. In Thai culture, rudeness is unforgivable. However, this time I distinctly felt the Lord caution me not to drink it. This was an awkward situation. As I tried to think around the problem, I concluded that by taking just one token sip I could avoid offence and get out of there as quickly as possible.

Later that night, I had a dream. Evil spirits appeared and said that I'd been in their temple eating their food. I had never had an evil spirit speak to me before and was very frightened. Ironically, my ambivalence was just a small picture of what the people hesitating to enter Christ were going through. There just wasn't a middle way. I confessed my disobedience to the Lord and asked his forgiveness, but I still didn't have peace.

The next Sunday, four of the men I was training to be leaders all came and confessed how they had sinned during the week. I realised that my own disobedience had caused the protective covering to be removed from all of us. I confessed my faults to them and we all prayed for God's forgiveness together. This seemed to clear the way for them but I personally fell back into bondage to the old familiar sense of failure and self-condemnation. This time, it piled up to the point where I decided to travel to Bangkok and meet with a prayer team to set me free. Graciously, the Lord met me in those sessions, and I returned to Phrabaht with a new sense of lightness in my spirit. We still had to contend with the spiritual realities of the situation, however, and though we prayed for God to have mercy on Noy's father, three months later he had a stroke that soon proved fatal.

From that point on, we devoted many hours each week in Bible study and discipleship with the believers. By now, two other missionary couples had joined Arlene and I, and there was a steady group of thirty believers. It was exciting and satisfying to see how much God had done. The church was a reality in Phrabaht!

On a personal level, I was due for a sabbatical, and was delighted when I got word that I had been approved to study at Victoria Bible College in Australia the following year. There was so much about spiritual breakthrough that I needed to explore! "I'll be back!" I reassured my team as I waved goodbye. I was already looking forward to returning once my sabbatical was over. But once again, God had other plans . . .

Chapter Nine

Darkness and Despair

My year-long sabbatical in Australia was exactly what I needed. Having enrolled in a Master's course for people who were engaged in fulltime ministry, it was a huge relief to spend time with like-hearted colleagues from my part of the world. I was delighted to discover that my experiences were similar to other people in ministry and that most of what we were learning backed up what God had already been teaching me. My thesis that year was about church growth, including strategic ways to promote further growth in the environment in which we served. As I presented the church in Phrabaht as a case study, I began to get insight into God's strategy to expand young church plants in Thailand.

During the year in Australia, I asked God constantly to show me what was on his heart for when I returned to Phrabaht. In response, he gave me a vision of a further two hundred people coming to Christ over the next three years. I could see that the church in Phrabaht was poised for even greater growth than we had experienced in the previous three years.

* * *

Then, just six weeks before I was due to return to Phrabaht, I received a letter from my leadership team that left me reeling. The letter said that Arlene, my fellow-worker was unable to work with me any longer because of 'theological differences'. This came as a real shock, because although I knew she didn't always agree with what I did, we had maintained a great relationship.

I knew that people were never the enemy, but this felt particularly difficult. The letter indicated that it was felt that Arlene should remain in Phrabaht but that I would be relocated to another town. I was grieved at the thought of losing this friendship—and then it dawned on me that my relationship with all the believers in Phrabaht would be lost because of this as well. Now I was not only grieved, but confused. "But I can't not return to Phrabaht!" I argued in my mind. "God has just given me a blueprint for the way forward!" Everything in me was determined to follow through with the vision I had been given.

In the end, however, the choice was not mine to make. My leaders were helpful and sympathetic but concluded I could not return to Phrabaht, but should instead go to Wiset, where another missionary couple had just been relocated, leaving a group of about twenty new believers bereft of the ones who had introduced them to the Lord. Was it God's intention that I share my gift of discipling with this infant church? Certainly, it helped that I was now fluent in the local language.

As I spent time with God and sought to make sense of this, he showed me many things that I needed to work through, including forgiving the leaders and trusting that God was in control. He also showed me that I had been proud in thinking I was the only one who knew how to minister in the power of the Holy Spirit. This had caused others to feel condemned. Thankfully, Arlene and I repaired our relationship fairly quickly, but I had learned a valuable lesson. I needed to release control into God's hands and trust him to grow the Church in his way. Now more than ever, he was taking me into a new situation where I would have to be totally reliant on him alone.

I was advised to start out in Wiset by meeting a Chinese couple who had been hosting this group in their home on the outskirts of town. Turning up at their home, my sense of apprehension only grew when I was set upon by a gaggle of ferocious geese right at the front gate. They attacked like guard dogs. "Anyone home?" My voice wavered as I called out. "Please call off your geese!" To my relief, the hosts rushed out, expressing a mixture of profuse apologies and warm welcome.

From there, they took me into their lounge, and over the next six hours, proceeded to download their previous experiences in four churches, and how none of those relationships had worked out. As I listened, my heart sank and I grew more and more discouraged. I couldn't shake the feeling in my spirit that things were not going to work out for me either. Eventually, my host asked me why I was so quiet. There was no way I could tell him how I was really feeling, so I simply replied that I was extremely weary. I finally said goodbye and got into a taxi to return to Lopburi, where I was staying, but as soon as the driver pulled away from the house, I began to cry and couldn't stop all the way home.

When my leader asked how the visit went, I burst into tears again as I related what had happened over the course of the day. I told him how strongly I felt that this new assignment was not going to work out well. He listened and then encouraged me to trust God. Next morning, he shared a great number of scriptures to encourage me that God *would* be with me. He told me I was a strong woman and that I would be able to cope. I certainly didn't feel like it, but knew I'd determined to honour my leaders and I determined once again to trust God no matter what!

A week later I moved to Wiset. I had arranged to stay temporarily with the couple I had previously visited. My little bedroom suite was conveniently outside and private, which suited me well—until I needed to go into the main house. To get inside, I needed to first call out for someone to rescue me from those hissing, honking geese. The other downside of the couple's hospitality was that they wouldn't let me do anything in return. Help with the dishes or sweep the floor? Contribute like any family member? Oh no! Their preconceived idea was that I would exist like a priestly monk in their home. In their mind, my duty was to pray and seek God and share the Word with them. To them, the word 'holy' meant keeping apart from mundane living.

The new Christians were underwhelmed by this newcomer for other reasons. Clearly, I was neither vivacious nor musical like my predecessors, and they soon lost their enthusiasm about worshipping together when they realised there would be no bright guitar playing to back them up. They were not particularly welcoming when I visited them in their homes either.

I found this very discouraging and soon felt myself coming under a similar kind of spiritual oppression to what I had experienced in Phrabaht. Truthfully, I was still grieving for the place and people I had left behind, and this made it difficult to function. I had determined to trust God no matter what, and every morning I walked and worshipped for up to an hour before even trying to meet the demands of the day. But it wasn't just grief I was dealing with. The spiritual atmosphere in Wiset was unlike anything I had encountered before. I had never felt rejection in Thailand the way I did in Wiset. On top of that, superstition was rife—and visible. The largest Buddha in Thailand stood in the grounds of a nearby temple, with a huge garden of grotesque concrete figurines graphically depicting the torments of hell.

During my first three weeks of living on the outskirts of Wiset, I had a growing sense of desperation. I called my mum in New Zealand, asking her to get the prayer team praying specifically and urgently. "Please tell them I can't live with this level of oppression!" I pleaded. Praise God, within half an hour of that phone call, the oppression lifted. It was a relief to recognise it as spiritual attack so much sooner than when I had first experienced a similar onslaught back in Phrabaht—and to actually feel the immediate effects of the prayers of God's people. I would never have made it without their speedy action.

He rescued me from my powerful enemies, from those who hated me and were too strong for me. They attacked me at a moment when I was in distress, but the Lord supported me. He led me to a place of safety; he rescued me because he delights in me.
Psalm 18:17-19

Eventually my hosts suggested I move into the heart of the market area, and set up a meeting place for the church there. "When you have twenty people coming like we had before, we will join you," they told me. My mind baulked at their words. How could I rebuild the church on my own? Nevertheless, I began looking for a place to rent. Rental properties in the market were scarce, and the only one I could find that seemed like a possibility was in a row of shop-houses, opposite the popular snooker club. Every shop in the row had one room above a ground-level shop guarded by a ubiquitous concertina iron grill door that let in air, cats and rats, but offered some security. An open drain flowed parallel to the shopfront. Incredibly I didn't even notice the sewage at first!

I went ahead and rented the premises, and once I'd set up home, three of the original believers began meeting with me on Sundays. Now I had a far more pressing dilemma to face—how would we get locals to come when two of those were leprosy patients and the third was one of their nephews who was intellectually challenged. Every Sunday morning we held a service, but there was always anxiety in my heart. What an inauspicious beginning! Surely this was getting off to a wrong start. I was also aware that we were being watched by the locals, and that we would likely be stuck with their judgment of us. I knew from experience that when those who were considered outcasts in society attended, no one else would want to come. At the same time, I deeply resonated with Jesus' heart for the outcasts. Jesus invited them in. Could my trust in God stretch to visualising them as angels in disguise?

I was greatly encouraged when we were joined by Itti, a

biker from Angthong, a town in the neighbouring district, who had made a profession of trust in Jesus. He brought his wife and son along too, and together they brought some sense of normality to our worship times. They were also eager to learn and grow. Not long after they started coming, Itti bought a car. One day he came and told me that he would like to be excused from church for three years until he'd paid off his car. My mind was filled with pictures of the sort of spiritual attack that came upon vacillating, interested people, and I feared for him. I shared with him how it was always wise to put God first and that God would honour him if he did so.

* * *

Adjoining my new home was a telephone call centre where a family lived with two young children. I would go there occasionally to make international calls. Mew, their eleven-year-old daughter was highly social. One lunch hour she brought her rice bowl into my home saying, "Rice doesn't taste nice when you eat it on your own!" She was like an angel sent from heaven. Little did she know how sad and lonely I felt, being in the market on my own and not knowing how to make contact with people. She was the answer to my request that God would provide a link person to introduce me to the market.

After this, Mew often came to eat with me. I began to teach her how to make bread, muffins and pizzas, and over time I taught her to speak English. She loved the attention and we quickly developed a strong friendship.

Three decades later I received an email from someone who had met Mew in North Thailand. All those years she had been searching for me, trying to find out where I was. Our online reunion was a delight for us both and she wrote, "At last I have received my miracle from God and been reconnected with you." I was greatly encouraged to know that seeds which had been planted long ago, even if they lie dormant many years, can still bear fruit.

Another time when I was planning to spend a day in prayer, I asked the Lord, "Please could you send someone to join me?" Within half an hour there was a knock at the door. I was so amazed when I opened it to find a fellow New Zealander! I didn't even know that Alan Bennett was back in Thailand, but sure enough, he was in Bangkok and had travelled early that morning to come and visit me. Once again, the Lord made sure I had a partner for a time of intensive intercession. We prayed and cried together and called out to the Lord to make an impact in the town of Wiset. Looking back, I can see that God always arranged someone to come and support me when it all seemed too much to endure!

It was much the same when a team of four Korean girls came to visit. When they sang together in harmony, my heart absolutely melted and I couldn't hold back the tears of sheer joy as I soaked in the fellowship of other believers. I was so grateful to God for sending them.

* * *

I loved to ride out into the rice fields on my bicycle early in the morning to get some exercise and to enjoy God's creation and spend time in worship. One day I returned home in a hurry needing to go to the loo. Rushing inside, I didn't notice a large snake coiled around the top of the floor-level, squat toilet until I had already disturbed it! The snake raised itself up and swayed as if ready to strike. Personal business forgotten, I raced over to the neighbour for help. He obligingly came in with a long stick and string noose. Slipping the noose over the snake's head, he picked it up, and carried it around to the back of the house. There he released it not far from my toilet drain hole! Being Buddhist, he wouldn't kill it. Now I worried that the snake could reappear at any time.

Once I got over my initial shock, I had time to reflect on the circular nature of spiritual attacks, and how necessary it is to claim the victory again and again . . . and again! Instead of blaming myself for setbacks, or looking for the weaknesses in others, I began to realise the need to close off any entry points of the enemy. For me, one of the areas I needed to deal with was the issue of rejection. During my first year in Wiset I had felt rejected by the couple who held themselves aloof from our little Sunday service and had started to query whether I really knew the power of the Holy Spirit! The growth was far too plodding in their eyes. The 'evidence' they hinted at was that I didn't make people fall over when I prayed for them and I didn't make them cry when they received communion. These visible signs of the power of God were starting to make an impact in Bangkok revival meetings of the time, and the news of and hunger for 'signs' spread fast through the more conservative provinces. Because of this, the initial group of Christians had been disinclined to continue meeting. To make it worse, having seen the Holy Spirit work so much in Phrabaht and so little in Wiset, I also felt rejected by God.

Sadly, with no one else nearby to talk this over, I had slid into the trap of believing the lie of the enemy. I spent lots of time trying to dig out whatever I had done to grieve the Holy Spirit. The amazing thing was that when I occasionally went back to preach and teach in Phrabaht, where we had seen God work in amazing ways, God empowered my ministry and the people were blessed. But when I returned to Wiset it was as though the heavens were brass. I had no idea why God worked in one town and not in the other. Why would the Holy Spirit pour out blessing in one situation and not in another? Mistakenly I had concluded that it must be me!

Again and again, I had allowed the enemy to condemn me rather than take a stand on God's promises. Still, I often felt as though God had abandoned me in Wiset. All I could do was cling to the promise of his presence even when I saw very little evidence of either his presence or his activity. I believed that because he had called me, he would remain trustworthy. He would be with me!

God has said, "I will never fail you. I will never abandon you." So we can say with confidence, "The LORD is my helper, so I will have no fear. What can mere people do to me?"
Hebrews 13:5-6

Eventually I was able to look at the situation more objectively, and concluded it must be the state of the spiritual soil that made the difference. Later, I was thankful for the nudge to shift into the centre of the market. I could even thank God for those geese catalysts! Although it had been tough going, I realised that staying on the fringes of the town would have been a waste of time. God had put me in the most visible part of town because he wanted me on the frontline of invading previously undisputed territory held by the enemy of souls.

Chapter Ten

Healing and Restoration

It had been many years since I had studied nursing, and any ambitions for my previous career had been left far behind. Still, my training was not wasted. In a wonderful way, God was continuing to tie the 'loose ends' of my life together. Now it had become clear to me that spiritual and physical health are often connected, and God had been preparing me to minister to both.

Realising our capacity was limited, a few of us had been praying that God would send someone who could train us in ministering to the emotional and spiritual needs of the Thai people. And yet I realised this was no small ask. Thai culture valued a calm and gracious exterior which involved constant suppression of churning emotions. With no process for dealing with their inner malaise, people often became sick with no physical cause. Interestingly, the Thai people were acutely aware of the link between physical illness and spiritual or emotional factors. Our newer missionary doctors were often taken aback by the perception of their clients. They could readily identify the cause of their physical symptoms.

What they didn't know, was how to deal with the escalating fear, grief or anger that was affecting their health.

* * *

How thankful I was when a couple from England came to Thailand with a desire to train twelve missionaries who could in turn, equip other missionaries and national leaders in personal prayer ministry. Having developed a method of helping believers deal with emotional wounds, sin, bondages and the occult, they were excited to pass on their approach.

I was one of twelve missionaries invited to participate in a series of training sessions to be held over the course of three years. I was excited as I approached the first session. As I watched them model how to listen to people's deep emotional pain and then invite Jesus into the situation, hope filled my heart. What a difference this would make in the lives of the Thai believers!

But my focus quickly shifted when the trainers insisted that as the first attendees, we needed to have our own needs ministered to first. I had never encountered counselling quite like this before, but I embraced it eagerly. Each of us were allocated two hours with the trainers—for the first hour, they simply listened as we shared some of our difficulties, and for the second hour they ministered to us, helping us break down strongholds that had formed over the years.

What a powerful time of personal breakthrough this was for me! I shared how in my early days in Wiset, the couple who hosted me had told me quite frankly that the Holy Spirit was not with me because people didn't break down in tears or fall down when I prayed for them, and how in my spirit I had agreed with them. Not only had I felt abandoned by people and was serving alone in Wiset, I struggled to see evidence of God's presence with me. "You're believing a lie!" they said with compassion. "You are not abandoned, Ginette; the truth is, the Holy Spirit is with you! He lives in you!" As the team followed the leading of the Holy Spirit, I began to see the pattern of self-condemnation I had lived with for many years. What a difference that one session made! I was filled with hope. Having dealt with self-condemnation most of my life, I was beginning to be set free!

During another prayer counselling session, God met with me in a deep way as I brought the shame and condemnation from the time I had been sexually abused as a child. *Was I willing to give up my hard-earned personal holiness and just receive Jesus' holiness?* This was like asking me to give away my security. It was very difficult to do. But having begun my healing journey, I was determined to trust the Lord. I was amazed to discover that God could set me free from the recordings of condemnation that had played in my mind for more than forty years, causing me to feel intimidated and even emotionally paralysed at times.

One of my most significant moments occurred during a ministry session with one of my colleagues. In prayer, she asked Jesus for a revelation of how he saw me. When he showed her a picture of me in a white dress with angels embroidered on it, I wept as I realised that Jesus had cleansed me and freed me from my shame. He never condemned me! The enemy was the one who filled my thoughts with accusation every time I tried to listen to God. The joy of being completely loved and accepted by God washed over me that day.

As our initial team of twelve missionaries were open and honest with each other, and as we ministered in listening prayer to each other's needs, a real sense of intimacy developed among us. It was the same when we ministered to our Thai fellow workers. As we dealt with our wounds, a growing camaraderie emerged. It was such a blessing to see God setting us free to enjoy him and to experience his power working through us.

From there, the ministry expanded. Soon, the Thai leaders began seeking their own healing, and in turn began ministering to those in their pastoral care. Some western missionaries expressed their doubts that the Thai would reveal their heartaches, so long repressed, in order to receive prayer ministry. However, we found that once they relaxed and realised they were safe and loved, they were able to acknowledge their hurts in the presence of Jesus.

One woman who came for one-on-one prayer was so distraught she couldn't speak. She just wept. I realised this was not normal grief, so I silently prayed, asking the Holy Spirit himself to come and minister to her. What an awesome experience it was for me to witness his transforming work in this woman's life! As she lingered in his presence, she saw Jesus take her in his arms when she was a baby and cuddle her. Then he washed her and dressed her in a new white dress. "We're going through the sky and he's taking me to heaven," she exclaimed. Jesus was showing her the home he had prepared for her! He went on to reveal the future he had prepared for her. Within the space of about an hour, this woman had become a completely different person! She became radiant as she told us her story. She had been sexually abused as a child. Then as a teenager she had been abducted by the communists, taken into the jungle and raped. Later, as a vulnerable widow living alone near the border, she was raped again. Shame overwhelmed her. She was completely broken by self-condemnation and despair. But now God had lifted the burden from her and revealed his love and acceptance! She glowed with joy. "Please tell my story wherever you go," she said, "so that people can know that if God healed me, he can heal anyone."

Over the years that followed, we were constantly amazed at how the Holy Spirit brought his love and healing touch as we ministered alongside him. Gradually, the church began to see themselves differently—no longer through Satan's twisted perspective, but as dearly loved children of God who had been made whole in Christ.

> *With my whole heart, with my whole life, and with my innermost being, I bow in wonder and love before you, the holy God! Yahweh, you are my soul's celebration. How could I ever forget the miracles of kindness you've done for me? You kissed my heart with forgiveness, in spite of all I've done. You've healed me inside and out from every disease. You've rescued me from hell and saved my life. You've crowned me with love and mercy.*
> Psalm 103:1-4 TPT

Pastor Pon was one of the first Thai leaders to join the healing ministry. She had experienced God setting her free from the emotional pain she had experienced as a child and releasing her to be the happy, joyful person God had always intended her to be. And so, when it was time for the ministry to be handed over to Thai leadership, it was Pon who was entrusted with overseeing and training the expanding local team.

* * *

The breakthrough I experienced on a personal level soon led to an amazing shift in my situation in Wiset when I met a teacher in the local high school. 'Mrs Peace', as she was known, was a devout Buddhist. She had observed that I was lonely and struggling to integrate into the community, and offered to help me by bringing her students to study English with me on Saturday mornings. Her husband was a teacher also. He was also the head of the education department for that province, and I was invited to teach English classes in their schools. This public endorsement quickly opened up further opportunities; when we offered to bring short-term teams from New Zealand to run English camps in regional schools, they were delighted.

My friendship with Mrs Peace and her husband was a real gift, and as we got to know each other, we found we had much in common. In the cool of the evenings, we would often head out for a special meal at the riverside, where we would talk about our lives and share our common values.

We had begun a genuine relationship, but as time passed, I longed to introduce them to Jesus. An opportunity arose some months later when tragedy struck at one of their schools.

Right before our English camp was about to start, one of the students took their own life, sending waves of shock and fear through the school community. The teachers were quick to respond by suggesting we cancel our upcoming English camp. *What if one instance of 'bad luck' led to another? Would the students even come to the school when no one knew how the spirit of the dead young person might reappear?* We assured the local students and staff that our team from New Zealand would be happy to sleep at the school the night before the camp started, in order to give the students and teachers peace of mind. Mrs Peace was shocked, but we gently explained that because of Jesus, we were able to live without fear. The camp did go ahead, and what a joy it was to see breakthrough—the students were able to see that Jesus had the power to protect them from every form of darkness.

The team from New Zealand had arrived just before Christmas, which also marked the start of the dry winter festive season in Thailand. This was always an ideal time to share Christ. In fact, the locals welcomed it. Together we put on a Chinese banquet for two hundred people on the street outside my shopfront. The civic wardens obligingly blocked off the street to traffic. Our team intertwined the courses with a concert of Māori songs and poi, bright musical items and a Christmas nativity play. With the aid of loudspeakers, many more than two hundred heard the gospel that evening.

My brother's children were part of this team from New Zealand. How thrilled I was for them to experience their own lives being used by God. My niece and nephews stayed on after the team left, as Mum and Dad were to join us for

Christmas. How I looked forward to their visit! Over the years since I had left New Zealand, they prayed for me daily and faithfully wrote to me every week, but nothing compared to seeing them in person. The minute they set foot in Thailand, they infused me with such joy and energy, springing into action as if they were one of the team. My Dad had a real passion for sales, and loved nothing better than to get out and meet people. After becoming a Christian, he had turned into an outgoing evangelist. Having discovered that Jesus alone was the Saviour who could heal him and deliver him from all his sins, he was unstoppable. Who wouldn't share such good news! Even the Thai language was no barrier to my dad. He exuded genuine interest and concern for everyone he met.

People were drawn to my mum as well. She soon won my Thai friends and colleagues over with her caring, compassionate and understanding heart, and they were delighted to be with her.

My parents' visits were a rich blessing to me also. They were the ones who knew and loved me more than anyone else. When issues arose that my teammates struggled to understand, my parents simply 'got it'. Even more importantly, their visits endorsed me in the eyes of the local community. Family networks are vitally important to the Thai people and they found it difficult to understand why a lone individual would come to their country. Without knowing my parents or siblings, how could they know who I really was? The fact that I was so wonderfully accepted by the Thai people is due, in no small part, to my parents' regular visits.

I was especially thankful to have my family with me that

year—and even more so when I received the awful news on Christmas morning that Itti, the young man from Angthong, had wrapped his car around a power pole and been killed! I left my parents in charge as visitors began arriving, and went to visit his wife in the temple where the body was lying. It was a very sad funeral. The weight of responsibility for people to truly enter into Christ and be eternally safe almost overwhelmed me.

Now that one team had come from New Zealand, more began to come. What a blessing this was for me! It had seemed almost impossible to witness and demonstrate the love of Christ when I was on my own in Wiset. For the first year I spent a lot of time seeking God, praying and believing him for a breakthrough just as we'd experienced in Phrabaht. Now I was seeing doors of opportunity swinging open in a way I hadn't seen before.

* * *

To that point, I had struggled with loneliness and rejection. But with the woundedness in my spirit now healed, I found myself eager for company. My leadership were quick to agree, and because there were no missionaries available to join me at the time, they encouraged me to look for a Thai colleague.

At the start of my second year in Wiset, I was delighted to unexpectedly meet up with a young woman I had discipled in Bangkok nearly ten years earlier. Dee had since completed her studies at bible college and had been involved in church planting. Now she was looking for a new ministry position, and was delighted to come and work with me. What a great match!

Dee soon joined me, but came under attack as soon as she arrived in Wiset. She was often overcome in her sleep by the spirits to the point that when she woke, she was paralysed and couldn't even call out for help. I knew that we needed to close any entry point to the spirits that tormented her, and as we prayed for deliverance and inner healing, God gave the victory!

It was exciting to have a companion to go out with on visits once again, and Dee was enthusiastic. However, after the first few outings she raised some pertinent questions. "How can you go out on the streets and try to talk with my people about Jesus when you don't know even know them?" she asked. "How would you like it if a Buddhist in New Zealand tried to convert you without having any relationship with you?" I could see she had a point. Dee also had a suggestion. "Why don't you get some formal qualifications to teach English? Then you could do something useful for the community." At first I felt a little put out by her comments, but a seed had been planted in my heart, and I started to explore the possibilities.

Over time, more missionaries joined us. This allowed the gospel to reach into more places, and I was grateful for their company. But despite having new colleagues and the excitement of expanding opportunities to share the gospel, I arrived at the end of my third year in Wiset feeling totally exhausted. I had approached my return to Thailand with a clear vision for Phrabaht. When it came to Wiset, however, I still had no real picture of what God had in mind. Devoid of a vision for the future, I began crying out, "I can't carry on like this, Lord. I need you to give me a new vision for the future."

God heard that prayer, and met me in an extraordinary way. Travelling in a van to South Thailand with Dee to visit her family, I was suddenly overwhelmed, and with tears pouring down my face, pleaded with God for help to carry on. In that moment, he gave me a vision of an English school with many classrooms, and young people from abroad coming to teach. I pictured using my experience in language and culture to oversee these teams and facilitate the classes. Suddenly, it seemed like a real possibility! I returned from our time away feeling refreshed and excited about what the future might hold.

* * *

I called my leaders to share my vision, knowing we would need to wait until after I returned from my scheduled visit to New Zealand later that year. I would focus on finishing up in Wiset and packing up my home in preparation for my departure.

But then, I received a telegram from home informing me that my dad was seriously ill and needed surgery. "Let's bring your home assignment forward," my leaders agreed. When a team from Australia requested to come right before my new leaving date, I replied, "You are very welcome to come—if you are willing to help me pack up the house as well!" With everything happening in fast motion, I had neither the presence of mind nor the capacity to do it all on my own.

What a gift it was to have this team to help me! I sorted my things into three piles and explained to them: these are to go with me, these are to be packed to stay, and these are giveaways—and that was that! Before I knew it, my home was not only packed up, but cleaned from top to bottom!

Now, with a few days to spare, I encouraged the team to visit Pon, the young church worker I had discipled during my second term in Lopburi. Pon had gone on to study at bible college and had since planted a church in Lopburi. Little did I know that as a result of that visit, a church in Australia would begin partnering with Pon, and that eventually, the Lord would lead her to pastor the church in Wiset. For sixty years, people in Wiset had heard the gospel but had gone on to truly follow the Lord only after they moved on to other places. Very few had made a clear-cut profession of faith while living in the town. A few years' later, under Pon's leadership, that pattern began to change.

* * *

During my years in Wiset, I had learned to survive by clinging to God and discovering a deep intimacy with him. One of the promises he gave me was from Song of Solomon:

> *"Who is this one? She arises out of her desert, clinging to her beloved. When I awakened you under the apple tree, as you were feasting upon me, I awakened your innermost being with the travail of birth as you longed for more of me"*
> *Song of Songs 8:5 TPT.*

I had learned that I needed to do more than simply rely on 'power encounters' to validate my relationship with Him, but to experience 'clinging to my Beloved'—to adopt a posture of total dependence on him as my divine helper and husband. I was stirred by his promise in return:

> *But then I will win her back once again. I will lead her into the desert and speak tenderly to her there. I will return her*

> *vineyards to her and transform the Valley of Trouble into a gateway of hope. She will give herself to me there, as she did long ago when she was young, when I freed her from her captivity in Egypt. "When that day comes," says the Lord, "you will call me 'my husband' instead of 'my master.'"*
> Hosea 2:14-16

I had learned to cling to him as my lover. He had created a deep hunger in me for intimacy with Him. He had taught me the power of love, forgiveness, and had given me the ability to bless those who had rejected me. I had also discovered that love truly is the most important of all the gifts (1 Corinthians 13:13).

* * *

My dad had already had surgery and was feeling better by the time I arrived in New Zealand. I enjoyed connecting with my family and friends, but my vision of running a language school was still fresh in my mind. With that purpose ahead of me, I had already enrolled in a course of study that would enable me to teach English professionally to students from non-English-speaking backgrounds. What a blessing it was to be able to attend classes at the same language school where my sister-in-law, Airini, was a teacher! She was a great help as I prepared for the final theory exams. Thankfully, I enjoyed the practical teaching components of the course, and did very well in them. With my new certification under my belt, I was able to gain six months formal teaching experience before returning once again, to Thailand.

Chapter Eleven

Back to Bangkok

After a full year in New Zealand, I felt ready and enthusiastic to return to Thailand. This time, I had a distinct sense that God was working 'all things together for good', and was excited when the leaders of my organisation encouraged me to pray about the possibility of teaching English in Bangkok — the city I had come to for language-learning more than two decades earlier. The details came together quickly when a Thai-led English language school requested help from native-English speaking teachers. I decided to join them for an initial one-year period.

* * *

I travelled into Bangkok's city centre once a week to teach English to a class of students. They were so motivated and enthusiastic. I was pleased to see what a great syllabus the school was using. The school had been started by Baptists many years earlier. They were well organised, had a great reputation, and they were keen to have our help.

Towards the end of that year, my agency approached the Baptists about the possibility of expanding into another area of Bangkok. Their director agreed, and with their expertise, we were able to set up our own branch of the school, and with their curriculum and infrastructure, we soon were accredited and were able to open our doors to students.

Located in a fast-growing suburb packed with young professionals, the opening of the new branch of the language school was met with great enthusiasm. Pastor Thongchai, the leader of the language institute, shared in his dedication speech how Peter and John had fished all night and caught nothing. "That's how it's been for many missionaries," he remarked. "One of the reasons is that we encourage people to 'change religions' without providing a safety net as they cross the huge chasm from one faith to another." He read from Luke 5:4-7:

> "Now go out where it is deeper, and let down your nets to catch some fish." "Master," Simon replied," we worked hard all last night and didn't catch a thing. But if you say so, I'll let the nets down again." And this time their nets were so full of fish they began to tear! A shout of help brought their partners in the other boat, and soon both boats were filled with fish and on the verge of sinking.

Pastor Thongchai believed that as we partnered together to give the community the English language skills they needed, we would in turn see a large spiritual harvest. He also had a personal encouragement for me. "For one year, don't make it your priority to share the gospel," he said. "Focus instead on building genuine relationships. When you do that, you will see genuine fruit!" This word gave me a wonderful sense of freedom. I had wanted to 'just preach the gospel' because I knew that's what people really needed. But God had been gently softening my heart. He showed me I had adopted a judgmental attitude towards other styles of outreach. Now I could see the wisdom in focussing on people's physical needs as well. Not only did it open up natural ways of connecting with local people, but by providing the language tuition the community needed, we were building bridges that would one day allow people to come to Jesus.

And it worked! A year later, a young man who had been unemployed and attending the English classes, turned up one day clean shaven and dressed nicely. "Why do you look so different today?" we asked. "Because I want to become a Christian," he replied. "I have experienced genuine love through you people and I decided it must be God's love." It was such an encouragement to see God at work through authentic, caring relationships.

About this time, I remembered a dream God had given me before the language school had opened. In my dream, I was heavily pregnant and gave birth to twin girls. It was so real that I awoke in shock, wondering how this could possibly happen. I realised God was showing me what was taking place in the spiritual realm—I understood that the one girl represented the language school we were setting up, and the other represented a church that God was going to bring to birth. The fact that they were girls told me that they were both going to reproduce and multiply. And that is exactly what happened.

My desire in setting up the school was that out of it, we could establish a new church plant in Bangkok. I wanted to work alongside a Thai pastor right from the start, so that the growing church would be safeguarded if the missionaries had to pull out for any reason. I knew it was much harder to introduce a national pastor once a church had become accustomed to western missionaries, and I recognised this was an even greater risk among our school community, where proficiency in the English language was considered a mark of success.

My prayer was answered when Pastor Sommai and Rusamee, with their young family, came to work with us. Pastor Sommai had very little English, which made it difficult at first, but he was willing to learn, and he always had a word from God to encourage us. Rusamee, his wife, brought a further sense of security when she established a nursery school to help supplement their income.

Now, I was fully released to operate in my strengths. Between teaching English and discipling believers in the local church, my life soon became a joyful whirl of activity. I was leading a great team of both Thai and Westerners, and each one was functioning in their own area of gifting. My goal was to have everyone working side by side as equal partners in the team. Being from a number of different cultures, however, I knew this would take time. While some were familiar with the concept of working as equals, for others it was more of a challenge.

And yet, our unity was strong. Soon our team was teaching classes on weeknights and Saturday mornings in order to meet the needs of workers as well as students. But the students had an insatiable hunger to learn English, and much to our continual amazement, they kept coming.

Over the next four years, over two thousand students

enrolled in our classes. But our aim was not only to teach, but to build long-term relationships and to plant a church. To aid that, we ran an English camp twice a year. This was a chance for our teachers and students to all get away and relax together. We would commence with English lessons on the Saturday, along with fun and games. Then on the Sunday we had a demonstration church service, also in English. Most of our students had never been to a church; now they had the chance to hear the gospel in a context that was comfortable for them. We also ran an English conversation club every second Friday night where we had games, testimonies and food.

Dee and Arlene, who had been serving in other parts of the country, had since come to Bangkok and were now part of the team who served in the language school. Dee and I rented a two-storied house, where for two months at a time, we hosted young people who came from abroad to teach English. We enjoyed hosting and discipling these young teachers, and they in turn were a great help in running camps and events as well as teaching classes. The Thai students loved meeting and connecting with people who couldn't speak their language. It was just as the Lord had shown me in the dream he had given me in the van in South Thailand.

Along the way, our team had been meeting for fellowship every Sunday afternoon. Gradually, as we invited the Thai to join us, and as young people came to know the Lord, a new church began to form. We called it Friendship Church. The church had been birthed out of the English school, but that changed two years later when we put up a sign, letting people know about our Sunday services.

The day after we put the sign up, a Muslim lady walked in off the street. She'd been looking in the area for two years for a church but could not find one. She had even been out on the streets looking for people who might be handing out tracts but couldn't find any. She said, "I want to become a Christian!" I was a bit taken aback and suggested she start by studying the Bible with us to make sure she understood. She answered, "Jesus is the Son of God, isn't he?" I said yes. "He died on the cross for our sins, didn't he?" Yes. "Then I want to become a Christian!" Pastor Sommai talked with her and invited her to discuss things again. The very next day she came back with her daughter. Both were determined to follow Jesus. For two years, God had been preparing them through Christian television programs. Now it was amazing to see them give their hearts to the Lord. This was such a gift from the Lord; one that was totally unexpected!

* * *

Back home in New Zealand, my mother was becoming progressively forgetful. It was during my last home assignment that I sensed something was wrong. My dad had noticed Mum's forgetfulness but had not associated it with any disease. I took Mum to the doctor, who suggested I had 'out-of-town-daughter syndrome' and recommended some tests. He told me that often a family member who has been away a long time, notices the changes more sharply than those who are always home. After a number of assessments, Mum was diagnosed with late-stage Alzheimer's disease. I could see that Dad had done an amazing job of caring for her, in spite of being in his mid-eighties. But he was very stressed, and not sleeping well at night. What should I do? God had called me to serve him in Thailand for life, but I'd told Mum and Dad five years earlier that I'd be willing to come home and care for them if there was ever a need. I could not decide what to put on the altar, ministry or parents, so I gave them both to God and acknowledged my dilemma: "I can't choose. Please show me clearly what you want me to do."

I ended up returning to Thailand, but within a few weeks Mum and Dad were both on the phone to me in great distress. They were not coping. I wrote to my brother and also to a dear friend and confidante to ask what they thought. Both of them replied, "We're glad you are asking—we believe you should be here for them." I found this very difficult to process. I had observed that single women were often 'requested' to return home in order to care for parents, and in many instances, it had become a subtle snare to stop a valid ministry. I wanted to avoid that trap, and asked God to guide me directly. Almost immediately, I read these words from 2 Samuel 7:

Go ahead and do whatever you have in mind, for the Lord is with you (v 3)

Are you the one to build a house for me to live in? (v 5)

The Lord declares that he will make a house for you (v 11)

Those words, although originally spoken by the prophet Nathan to King David, resonated in my own spirit. The OMF leadership was in agreement. God was releasing me from my work in Thailand.

What a delight it was to hear that already God had prepared three new missionaries to take my place! Having just finished their own training and orientation, they were ready for their first assignment—just as I was about to leave. And so it was, that with a real sense of closure, I was able to say goodbye to my friends and to the land I had come to love.

Chapter Twelve

COMING HOME

As soon as I arrived back in Christchurch, I rented a flat within easy walking distance of Mum and Dad. What an amazing opportunity it was to finally be able to reciprocate the deep commitment they'd given me over so many years. But the first six months were difficult. Mum had begun to wander at night, and Dad was struggling with lack of sleep as he cared for her night and day. I longed to settle down, but the transition home proved harder than I'd imagined. I felt like a misfit in my own country. New Zealand culture made me feel lost. I had missed a quarter-century of national life. I didn't even know how to use a bank card. Going to the supermarket was exhausting—none of the brands were familiar, and the variety overwhelmed me. Every day I was meeting new people, but I had no idea how to start conversations with them. Their lives were nothing like the life I'd just left behind. Even returning to church left me feeling disoriented. I listened to the Sunday sermons, but the illustrations were often unfathomable to me. It was as if I was understanding the English, yet missing the message.

How grateful I was for the immediate loving acceptance of my home church—and for the support groups around the

South Island, who had prayed for me faithfully over many years. After each of their visits to Thailand, my parents had personally visited the OMF prayer groups back home. Hearing their enthusiastic updates, they not only prayed, but they had shared in the joy of answered prayer. In every way, they had been part of my work.

But churches had supported me as well, and for the first six months after my return, I was required to visit them on Sundays to thank them for their support and to give a report on what God was doing in Thailand. I found this excruciatingly difficult. Preaching filled me with fear. My old insecurities returned every time I was asked to speak. I often felt paralysed and had no idea what to say. Once I was due to preach, but fear had taken over. In tears I called my sister-in-law, Airini. Immediately, she came to my house and prayed until I was filled with the peace of God.

My brother and his wife were a blessing in so many ways during that time. Every Sunday, they had me over to their home for a meal. More than anyone, Edwin and Airini helped me understand my own culture, and grounded me with their loving acceptance when I often felt I was lurching from crisis to crisis.

Six months into my re-entry, my mum fell and broke her wrist. For Dad, this was a moment of decision. Was it time to place Mum in a nursing home? But I had another suggestion. "What if she comes to live with me?" I said to Dad. "Then you can have a good night's sleep, you can come and enjoy your meals here, and you'll be able to take Mum out anytime you want." Dad agreed, and the arrangement turned into a blessing for us all. Dad got the rest he needed, along with plenty of time with Mum, which allowed me to pick up part-time work in a local language school and begin to settle into a routine. Mum didn't wander at night any more. And I was thrilled to do something practical for my precious family. I noticed how my mum relaxed when I gave her my full attention or just sat and held hands with her, and how it distressed her when I worked on my computer.

For me, this was a time of enjoying my restored identity both as a child of God—and as a loved part of my earthly family. Over the years, my greatest fear had been not 'getting it right'. I worried about not being good enough or acceptable to God, of never doing enough to please God—and as a result I was never sure he really loved me. Throughout my childhood I had felt like I had to work hard to keep the peace in my family, and could never relax for fear of making things worse. But over my years in Thailand, God had healed my heart and imparted a new sense of identity. Now I was able to serve in my family, not with a sense of duty but with the confidence and joy of simply belonging.

> *You did not receive the "spirit of religious duty," leading you back into the fear of never being good enough. But you have received the "Spirit of full acceptance," enfolding you into the family of God. And you will never feel orphaned, for he rises up within us, our spirits join him in saying the words of tender affection, "Beloved Father!" For the Holy Spirit makes God's fatherhood real to us as he whispers in our innermost being, "You are God's beloved child!"*
> Romans 8:15-16 TPT

Having my mum living with me was a time of real healing for us both. We'd always been very close, and she had missed me greatly during my twenty-three years in Thailand. Now I was thankful for the opportunity to spend time with her and give her the loving attention she needed. I realised just how much of a difference it made when as a family we decided to place Mum in respite care for two weeks. I took the opportunity to make a short trip back to Thailand, but on my return, we found Mum had visibly deteriorated. She appeared vacant and distressed, and it took a full week after bringing her back home, for some semblance of normalcy to return.

One day soon after, my dad came to take Mum out while I went off to teach English. In the middle of class, I received a call to say that Mum had collapsed and was being taken by ambulance to the hospital. Leaving the class, I hurried to the hospital, praying that God, in his mercy, would take my mum to be with himself. I had always prayed that God would give my parents a quick and painless death. What a relief it was when, on arriving at the hospital, I was told that Mum had indeed passed away. I don't think she ever knew what happened to her—she had suffered a massive stroke and died as she collapsed into Dad's arms. How kind of God to allow Dad to be with her!

I thought of how that morning Mum had come upstairs to my bedroom and said, "Where's my darling?" Then she slipped into the single bed with me to enjoy time together like we had done in my childhood. Being a bit squashed, I soon rose to prepare breakfast. I'd have lingered more if I'd realised that we only had a few hours left together on this earth. Now

Mum had a new body and a new mind! Knowing she was completely healed, I had nothing to grieve that day. Mum was in a far better place, forever with Jesus.

* * *

After Mum died, I was at a loss as to what to do other than continue part time English teaching. And yet, I struggled to find joy in it. My class of ten Asian students was only interested in learning just enough of the language to gain a visa. My heart wasn't in it either. The day I returned to teach after Mum's funeral was unbearable, and so I resigned. What a relief that was! God gave me a lovely promise for the season to come:

> *He brought me out into a spacious place; he rescued me because he delighted in me.*
> Psalm 18:19 NIV

Now I could focus on enjoying precious time with Dad. Although he continued to live in his own flat, he came to my home every night for our evening meal. The next three years turned into a wonderful time of healing for both of us as I learned to show my dad the same unconditional love that I had so easily shown Mum. This was not automatic after the enormous rifts in my youth, but we grew closer over that time, and grew to appreciate our different personalities. Eventually, however, Dad decided to move into an aged care home. As an extrovert, he loved the community atmosphere. He was a skilled photographer and would capture various events, get the photos printed, and give them to the delighted recipients. Dad also read to residents who were blind or unable to get out. When he offered them a choice of a book about heaven or another book, most wanted to read about heaven. Often by the second or third chapter, they'd ask, "How can I make sure I can go to heaven?" and as a result, Dad had the privilege of leading many to Christ. He also continued driving his car and loved coming to my place to help in the garden or even occasionally cook himself some lunch if I wasn't there. This was home away from the home for him.

At ninety-one, Dad was eating a meal when something snapped in his jaw. From that point on, he had trouble eating; soon he became noticeably fragile. Sitting with him as he began to slip in and out of consciousness, I noticed how his strength rallied with the anticipation that he would soon be with Jesus. One day he suddenly put his hands out, and I knew that now was his time to go. "Jesus is waiting for you Dad, and Mum is waiting for you too," I assured him. "You don't have to wait; you can go now." With that, he took one final breath and passed peacefully. What a glorious experience it must have been for him to leave his aged body and arrive in heaven! My dad had always loved adventure, and I could easily imagine him exploring the universe with Jesus with his youth renewed and his glorified body completely whole.

I often marvel that God restored our family and that because we have all placed our trust in Jesus, we will meet again. I never deeply grieved the loss of my parents, because of the thrill of knowing that they are in a better place. And whenever I feel bereft, I cling to Jesus' promise in John 14:18 (TPT): "I will never leave you helpless or abandon you as orphans—I will come back to you!"

***

God had done a remarkable work of healing in my life during my years in Thailand. However, my pervading sense of unease in social situations persisted even years after coming back to New Zealand. Feeling bogged down in brokenness and failure, I couldn't shake the deep-seated belief that I would never be able to serve God again. It wasn't until a local chaplain helped me discern the true nature of my grief that I began to see a way forward. She pointed out that I had never really processed the grief of leaving Thailand—in fact, I hadn't worked through a lot of the trauma I had experienced as I struggled to meet the expectations and reintegrate into New Zealand life. What a relief it was to realise that I wasn't inadequate, or a failure. I was actually experiencing burnout.

"What do you like to do to relax?" the chaplain asked me. I found this an odd question—and one to which I had no immediate answer. "I don't know," I replied. "I've never taken time to relax from what needs to be done." When she suggested I might like to explore what I would enjoy doing—like taking walks, visiting a cafe with friends, or swimming—I felt the weight lift off my shoulders. I was being given permission to slow down and enjoy being on the journey of life! That simple suggestion unlocked something in my mind, and opportunities began to open up ahead of me. I realised that my parents' wide network of friends had become my own!

As I began to appreciate the blessing of friendships and new activities, fresh opportunities began to open up. At last, I was experiencing the joy of relational living! It was a particular blessing, however, when a new friend showed up in my life.

Having spent many years of her life in a painful situation from which she and her husband had recently emerged, Elizabeth could identify with much of my journey—including my sense of failure. As we shared our stories and lifted each other up, we discovered a rich connection. We both loved the Lord and had experienced his healing work in our lives. As we discovered our shared desire to serve the Lord, God led us together into a new season of discipleship and ministry. What a blessing to have a kindred-spirit as we partnered together!

New joys opened up to me in my home church as well, when my pastors, who had supported me through all my years in Thailand, invited me to be part of the leadership team. At first, I was reluctant, but they assured me I didn't have to do anything, other than be part of the team and receive their love. I couldn't believe the amazing fun and fellowship we enjoyed together! I had forgotten what real Christian fellowship and acceptance was like. Even our days of prayer and planning were cocooned in an environment of relaxed affirmation and encouragement. After several years of mainly observing, I began to believe that I still had something to contribute.

A further opportunity arose when the local OMF representative resigned and I was asked to take over the role of South Island Coordinator. What a joy it was to serve within New Zealand in the mission I loved. I accepted on the condition I could incorporate my growing ministry of discipling into the role. This turned out to be a good mix. Over the years that followed I was able to mentor many young people who were interested in missions, and see them sent out on short term assignments. I also helped lead nine-month discipleship courses for mission teams in a variety of churches, and often had the privilege of leading these teams to Thailand.

And, I had the chance to come alongside returning missionaries as they encountered their own re-entry difficulties. What a need this was! As one person wryly commented to me, "We had been taught to surrender to God and to serve, but we'd never been taught to survive!" Now I could be the one to offer a listening ear. For many of them the isolation of living overseas had exacerbated the 'bruising' that had not been addressed prior to going to the mission field. Some of them had, like me, found themselves unprepared for the spiritual dynamics they faced. More than anything, they needed to be reminded that our worth is not dependent on where we have served or anything we may have achieved. Instead, we must apply the truth of Romans 8:1(TPT):

So now the case is closed. There remains no accusing voice of condemnation against those who are joined in life union with Jesus the Anointed One.

This is the key to victory over the lies of the enemy! What a joy to know and impart the truth of our identity, that we are the beloved children of God, no matter what.

EPILOGUE

Despite its strong start, the language school did not continue as expected. Just five years after it opened, the OMF leadership made the call to close our branch of the school, as they felt it had accomplished its task. This came as a terrible blow to those of us who taught there, and it particularly saddened me, as I always believed that the way we functioned as a team in love and unity would be reflected in the church that was simultaneously being birthed. But God had another perspective.

One day, as I was out walking with a friend, God drew my attention to a tree that had been cut down. Already the stump had begun to sprout again. As we smiled at the tree's stubborn persistence, a scripture came to mind:

> *Even a tree has more hope! If it is cut down, it will sprout again and grow new branches. Though its roots have grown old in the earth and its stump decays, at the scent of water it will bud and sprout again like a new seedling.*
> *Job 14:7-9*

The truth is that ministries come and go, but God's work continues to flourish. Recently, I heard that Aunty Jian, who must have been at least seventy years of age, had moved to another town where she began witnessing. This led to a church being established there—in fact, they have recently opened a second church building!

Another woman, who was illiterate and an alcoholic, had a desire to know Jesus. I used to go and teach her the Bible, and her two granddaughters who lived with her would also sit and listen. When she gave her life to Jesus, God delivered her from alcoholism. On seeing what God had done, her two granddaughters also believed. Today, one of them is a leader of the Phrabaht Church, along with her husband whom she led to the Lord.

As for Pon, she now pastors the small church in Wiset. Wiset remains a spiritually resistant town, and the attacks are relentless, and yet recently we heard that seven people came to faith there in one week. What an encouragement to know God has given Pon such a vision for this city. She now oversees many of the churches in the region and travels widely to encourage them.

Friendship Church has also flourished. Once the scaffolding of the English classes was removed, the Holy Spirit was poured out in a mighty way on the local workers. When I left Thailand in November 2001, there were about twenty local believers. Today, there are more than three hundred — as well as eighteen 'daughter' churches that have been birthed under Pastor Sommai's leadership. He went on to complete his doctoral studies in theology, and now runs an online school, training Thai pastors to be church planters. He called me earlier this year to invite me to a special occasion — the dedication of a new Friendship Church centre with a seating capacity of five hundred people!

The reality is, that as missionaries we are only ever the scaffolding. It is God who builds his church. He alone knows when it is strong enough to stand on its feet in the local environment; he knows when it is time to remove the scaffolding.

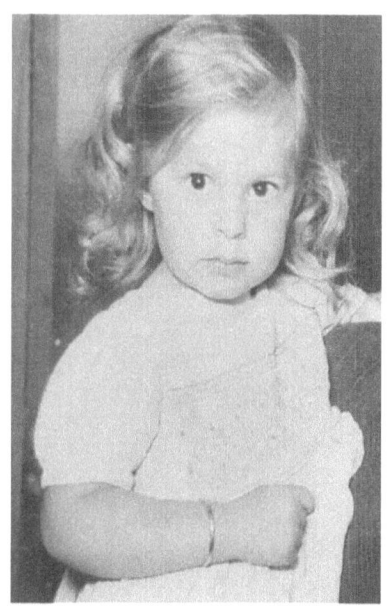

Ginette at three years old

Ginette, nursing at Christchurch Hospital (age 21)

Manorom Christian Hospital, where Ginette had expected to work in Thailand.

Setting out from the house Ginette shared with Barbara in Lopburi

Arlene (left) and Ginette in Phrabaht, 1989.

The Phrabaht church in front of Ginette and Arlene's home after one year.

With Arlene Sorensen outside our house and first church in Phrabaht.

Phrabaht Church meeting in a school hall after three years.

Sunday morning church service in Wiset.

Ginette teaching Mrs Peace's English students in Wiset.

Ginette and her parents in typical Thai dress, specially provided by Mrs Peace for their first Christmas in Wiset.

The Kiwi team performing a Māori dance during the Christmas outreach banquet in Wiset, 1994.

Pastor Pon (front row, second from right) with the church she re-established in Wiset, 2014.

Pastor Sommai (left), Ginette and Arlene (middle) with the Bangkok English camp students. Taken in 2001, a few months before Ginette's return to New Zealand.

Ginette visiting with Pastor Sommai (Friendship Church) and his wife in Bangkok.

First meeting in Friendship Church's 500-seat auditorium, established by Pastor Sommai (in white shirt, front centre).

Beginning of 2021. Meeting at Friendship Church with physical distancing possible.

Ginette, 2021 at home in Christchurch, New Zealand.

To get in touch with Ginette, please email:
nomatterwhat315@gmail.com

www.ingramcontent.com/pod-product-compliance
Lightning Source LLC
Chambersburg PA
CBHW031252290426
44109CB00012B/553